# O1 Goes Trekking

Introducing
**'SHE WHO MUST BE OBEYED'**

The Amigo treks to Mt Everest Base Camp

KETAN JOSHI

## INDEX

| | |
|---|---|
| Enter SHE WHO MUST BE OBEYED | 5 |
| The first trek - Harishchandragad | 47 |
| Off to Nepal | 87 |
| The trek starts | 118 |
| Deorali to Trakshindo | 138 |
| Trakshindo to Phakding | 167 |
| Phakding to Dingboche | 190 |
| Dingboche to Lobuche | 212 |
| The top of the world | 235 |
| More adventure! Chola pass and Gokyo | 257 |
| The end of the trek - Namche, Lukla | 276 |
| Lukla to Kathmandu | 291 |

**Prologue -**

**enter She Who Must Be Obeyed!**

One of the side effects of writing travelogues is the strange people you come in touch with.

I had written an account of an interesting trip I had done - a solo unplanned trip to the Kumbh Mela in Allahabad. (Check out 'One Man Goes Backpacking') I had run away from work to go and see the Kumbh - total AWOL stuff...If I had been in the army they would have put me on the brig or ironed me in the claps...or whatever it is they do to guys who vanish from their posts without leave.

The whole trip had been an exercise in Serendipity - I had wanted to go to the Kumbh mela, but I had no money, no holidays and no clue as to how to go about getting there - but suddenly the stars had aligned and things had clicked into place. Out of the blue, I had got an invitation to attend a job interview with a company in Delhi - and that gave me a free ticket to Delhi. After a rather strange job interview, I went to the New Delhi train station and took a train to Allahabad - I had no ticket...or rather, no reserved seating …so I had bought an 'open' ticket and piled on to a train - and since there was to place to lie down or even sit - made the journey sitting on the floor of the train - outside the toilet - and had nearly frozen to death in that ghastly North Indian winter. Brrr!

But I survived and made it to the mela, and hung out with pilgrims and grim Naga sadhus and partaken of the Maha Kumbh mela. I went to Benares and stayed on the banks of the Ganga, in a hotel made out of a refurbished cowshed. I took a holy (and very chilly) dip in the Ganga and - hopefully - washed away all my sins, and smoked ganja on the ghats with the boatmen and had a great time!

When I got home I wrote a mail about my adventures and sent it off to some friends - and those guys forwarded it to their friends and so forth, and it went viral. This was a long time ago, before the emergence of blogs and social media - so the only way things went viral was by people forwarding emails to each other.

And this email-forwarding put me in touch with the strange people - or rather - Person - or rather - Personage - about whom I had mentioned earlier.

One friend of mine - a bespectacled nerd called Saurabh Tiwary - sidled up to me and said 'Er...um…'

I waited expectantly, but he seemed to be a bit stuck.

'Er...Um…' He repeated and again stopped to collect his thoughts. He also turned red and mopped his brow. I noticed that he was actually sweating! Tiwary was a Materials management guy, which is a fancy word for someone who shouts at truck guys and vendors for a living. What had gotten him sweating?

'Er...Um…' he repeated for the third time, and squared his shoulders and seemed to affirm to himself that he was a man, a strong man, a Tiwary - and was not afraid of anyone. 'That Kumbh mela adventure mail of yours...er...um…'

'Yes?' I asked, trying to prompt him 'Did you like it?'

'Er...yes...I did. In fact, I ...er...forwarded it to someone.'

'Oh...OK.' I said 'I hope he likes it.'
'SHE.'
'Eh?'
'Not he, SHE.'
I was shocked. Tiwary knew girls? Who knew? I had thought that the only girls he knew were made of bits and bytes. Or imaginary ones. But I didn't want to wound him by expressing these thoughts. I decided to humour him.

'Oh? Ah? Well...I hope she liked it.'
'Not she. SHE.' his sensitive ears had picked up the difference in the capitalisation.
'Eh?'
'SHE WHO MUST BE OBEYED!'
'Eh? Who? What? Where?' I was totally

foxed.

'Bharathi!' he said, in a low voice, looking wildly here and there, like a hunted animal.

'Er...Vande Mataram?' I replied doubtfully, thinking that he had gotten some patriotism mania or something.

'Eh?' Tiwary was foxed.

'You said something about Bharat Mata, so I replied - Vande Mataram.' I explained.

'Arre...not Bharat Mata! Bharathi! She is the factory commercial manager at our Goa plant.'

'Ah?'

'She is a terror in the plant' Tiwary whispered to me. 'Even the Factory head jumps a foot on hearing her name!'

'Ah?'

'That is why SHE is called SHE WHO MUST BE OBEYED!'

'Ah?'

-----

This Bharathi, I learnt, was a keen traveller and used to write mails about her travels and mail them to friends, just as I had done. The difference was of scale - I had done two trips, while hers were without number.

One day, I heard that she had quit her job! The story went that she went to her boss and told him that she is resigning.
'Oh?' he said, no doubt restraining the urge to turn handsprings and dance around naked throwing flowers out of a hat. 'Er, found a better job which pays more?'
'No, nothing like that.' SHE replied
'Oh? Er...then...getting married and moving to your husband's city?' he said, no doubt repressing a pang of pity for that unfortunate spouse. Thoughts of a female Preying Mantis ripping the head off a male and eating it as a refreshing snack after copulation must have passed through his

mind.

'No' she replied scornfully. 'The man I marry will be a prince among men! An Adonis! A male Pygmalion!'

'Pygmalion was indeed a male, I believe...' the boss ventured to say, but shrivelled as SHE turned a fiery gaze on him. 'But never mind...er...heheheh...so, if not for a job and not for a mate, then why are you quitting?'

'I have decided to quit corporate life and travel the world!' she announced calmly.

'WHAT?' This was way back in 1999, and such thoughts had never entered anyone's head in India. Getting a job and making a salary was the holy grail - and the thought of anyone voluntarily stepping off the treadmill was something unimaginable. The boss reeled and clutched his forehead as his whole value system and world view quivered before his eyes. 'WHAT? QUITTING A JOB...TO GO ON A

HOLIDAY?'

'Yes. I thought about it. Before I get married and get saddled with men and babies and mothers in law and what not, I will revel in my freedom. I will climb mountains. I will sail the seas. I will go backpacking all over the world. I wil live a life far beyond what you mere mortals can ever dream of!'

The factory manager's head was about to burst. He couldn't imagine anyone leaving a steady job and a burgeoning career to do something as frivolous as travel. He came from a generation which had just emerged from the depredations of British rule and valued job security and steady employment above all else.

The wolf had never actually been to his personal door, but his earlier generations had heard it howling now and then at the edge of the village, and indeed had seen the wolf tear friends and acquaintances apart. This generation was one which valued hard work - they prided itself on never ever taking a vacation and prestige was counted in number of paid holidays not availed of! A steady income was their Godhead. It was like a survivor of a horrendous famine meeting a dieter who has decided to - voluntarily - eat as little as possible. Incomprehensible.

The only holiday they thought of taking were for births, deaths and marriage - and perhaps a pilgrimage. And here was a little scary titch of a girl babbling about leaving a good steady job - for no reason apart from to roam about like a hobo.

'But are you sure? What will happen to your career after such a long break?'

Bharathi looked him straight in the eye and

made him wilt. 'If I stay in this job, then I might become an office-going money-grubbing politicking corporate creep like you!'

There was nothing more said after that. He quietly accepted the resignation, and only requested that she stay on until her replacement could be found. Bharathi was OK with that - she would be getting a couple of months of salary, and would be able to dispose of her personal belongings and plan out her travels.

I read with fascination her e-mails describing her sabbatical - she first started by doing some local travel…by local, I mean travel in India.

She started by going to the Lakshadweep islands - a chain of islands on the western side of India - while still working off her pending holiday balance with the company. I read with fascination how she went to Cochin, and then took passage on the rickety ship M V Tipu Sultan to go to the islands. She went hopping from island to island as part of the Tipu Sultan cruise, and went snorkelling in the Arabian sea. It was her first fore-taste of unemployment ever - as she had gotten a pre-placement offer from a company while still doing her MBA and hence had never ever had that unpleasant sensation of being adrift and jobless.

After the official last day on her job, she kicked the dust of employment off her shoes - figuratively speaking - and spent some time getting rid off all her worldly possessions, like the Buddha casting away his garments before setting out to become an ascetic.

Then she packed what was left of her possessions in a backpack - like a snail or tortoise or something - and started northwards to the mountains. She stopped at Ranthambore tiger sanctuary - and saw no tigers at all. (Which tiger would dare to come near her? Till date she has never seen a tiger. Ha!) Then she dropped into Delhi and scared the pants off the Prime Minister - who was so scared that Bharathi will come to him and upbraid him about the state of the country, that he ran off overseas and didn't come back until the secret service assured him that she had only come to meet some friends and anyway she had already left for Haridwar.

Haridwar was anyway a magnet for all these ascetic type people who have left home and hearth - and they left Haridwar as well when she came. They probably ran away in droves - screaming in fear. But they had no cause to fear - Haridwar was only a stopover for her - her destination was the Indian Ski Resort of Auli, in Uttarakhand.

I had no idea that India has a ski resort - complete with ski lifts and whatnot - until I read about it in her mails. (Yes, I know…I am an ignorant fellow) It has some very nice slopes and there is a Government-run Ski resort which conducts a training course for skiers. She did a week long course there, and bowled over all the other participants - no, really bowled them over, by ramming into them while skiing - and left them black and blue and bruised all over. When the skiing was closed due to too much snow (sounds like a contradiction in terms, doesn't it) she would grab some hapless soul and force them to go trekking with her, and they visited the nearby hot spring of Tapovan.

After the Skiing course was over, she went back down to Delhi and probably closed her eyes and stabbed a finger on the map and saw that she was stabbing Bhutan (sounds a bit gory if you say it like that) and decided - Bhutan - here I come!

She ordered an old friend to come to Bhutan with her - he was a huge bearded bengali who looked like the Abominable snowman, but he also trembled with fear and saluted and said 'Yes Ma'm' and reported for the trip as commanded. She went to Calcutta from Delhi, and they took a flight to Paro - the only airport in that little Himalayan kingdom.

Bharathi was planning an all-out assault on Bhutan, and was planning to traverse it from stem to stern! (Is that the right expression?) Bhutan is a very expensive place to visit for foreigners - they have to pay USD200 per day per person to enter Bhutan, and this eye-watering cost restricts their visitor numbers and keeps out all the poor backpackers.

But Indian citizens do not need a visa - or even a passport - to enter Bhutan. But they are restricted to only some parts of the country. Well, most of them are - but Bharathi sneered at such restrictions.

They went for a 5 day trek in Bhutan - and they had to bargain and beg and plead with a Bhutanese tour operator to get a porter and stuff, because obviously the tour guy wanted USD 200 per day per person. But finally they managed to beat him down to a reasonable sum and booked a trek to Jhomolhari base camp with a guide and horse handler and what not. Bharathi had ambitions of doing the premier trek of Bhutan - the legendary 22 day 'Snowman trek' but that costs 4,400 USD per person!

Her bearded Bengali Yeti companion went back to Calcutta after the trek, and Bharathi continued in Bhutan - shocking the populace who clearly were not used to solo Indian women travellers outside the tourist circuits - especially ones who looked like dangerous little wolverines, apt to attack and bite if enraged. She travelled by public transport and explored the various 'Dzongs' - Bhutanese forts - and made her way eastwards across the country. Her permit actually ...er...permitted her to go only till Bumthang, in the centre of the country - but she decided that it was only a grubby piece of paper issued by some shiftless bureaucrat and should be treated with utter disdain. She met a french photographer who had been appointed by the royal government to photograph the country and tagged along with him, pretending to be in his entourage. The cops used to be so impressed by the Royal permit that they didn't question the presence of this little creature with him - and she managed to sneak her way to the border village of Samdrup Jonkar! The guards were very hassled that she had made it all the way there without a permit, but she flashed her eyes at them and they wilted and allowed her to enter Assam, India - no doubt very glad to see the back of her.

I could just imagine the telephone conversation
'Saar…she doesn't have permit saar …but she wants to leave the country…'
'Let her go …at once!' (wipes brow)

She made her way back to Delhi, and now decided to travel through Garhwal - the Himalayan region in Uttaranchal, India. She took an overnight bus to Rishikesh, and then another day-long bus to Joshimath. Both are long and bone-jarring journeys, and she tolerated them with dreams of enjoying trips to the the various high and holy places in the mountains… the four holy 'dhaams' and the 'Valley of flowers' and Hemkunt sahib gurudwara of the Sikhs and so on. But when she reached there, she came to know that most of these roads are still closed due to snow!

'Gah!' she said. 'Damn the snow! Full speed ahead! En Avaunt! Excelsior!'
'But the roads will be closed, madam!' the locals said, and quailed when SHE glared at them.
'Damn the closure! I will melt the snow with my third eye if required! I have come, I shall see and I shall conquer!'
She found a bus to take her to Govindghat, which is the roadhead for the trek to the Valley of Flowers. She started the trek alone

and wound her way to Phulna, which is the halfway point to Ghangriya - the starting point of the trek to the Valley of Flowers. It was dark when she got there, and there was no way to go forward alone in the dark, so she stayed with a family there, who were most intrigued to find a solo Indian female doing the trek when the roads were not yet open.

The next day she set out alone to Ghangriya - and she was completely alone! She didn't find a single person on the trail - it was totally deserted. She reached Ghangriya and finally came to a halt - the trails were covered in deep snow and there was no way to go any further. But it was extremely beautiful and she felt totally vindicated in doing the walk alone. She turned back and walked all the way to Phulna, and scared the pants off a villager who was shocked to see a small creature all alone on the mountain.

'Goblins! Orcs! EEEEEK' he shouted, and ran off.

Then she went back to the road head and took a bus to Joshimath - which is the base village for the Badrinath temple, and regaled herself with seeing a folk festival and play there. She was the talk of the town and become came to rubberneck at the 'small engineer' who had walked to Ghangriya alone.

The next day she came to know that there was a truck at 7 AM which ferried labourers to the Badrinath road who would be employed by the army to clear the path of snow and mud. She got a lift on that truck, inspite of the deep reservations of the army people, and managed to make her way to Badrinath temple - deep in the hills. The road was pretty perilous and they had to stop a couple of times to shove boulders off the road. That is to say - the others did the shoving and pushing - and she did the screaming and shouting.

But she had reached Badrinath! The whole place was deserted and she was the only Indian tourist there! She enjoyed the fantastic views, took a bath in the hot springs and enjoyed having the temple to herself.

Soon the news got around that a crazy little South Indian female had landed up there, and homesick South Indian soldiers made a beeline to meet her and speak to her in Tamil and Telugu. They were very happy to meet her and they fed her a nice meal from their canteen, and ensured that the truck driver dropped her back to Joshimath in the evening.

The next day she made another long and bone rattling bus trip to Gaurikund - the roadhead for the holy Kedarnath temple, and became an instant celebrity again as the first Indian tourist of the season. Again the cops were very chary of allowing her to trek to Kedarnath - it was a long trek - 14 Km up the mountain. The road had not been cleared and would be totally deserted, and she was a single female. But she begged and pleaded and nagged and blandished - and finally they agreed to allow her to ascend the mountain. A couple of policemen were doing a routine visit to Kedarnath and she was ordered to go with them. The views were fantastic - and the had to walk through 3 feet of snow at the end!

Everyone was very impressed with her stamina and courage and the head cop plied her with delicacies from his hometown, and the hotel owner fed her dinner from his home and refused to charge her anything. She almost wept with joy at the love being showered on her - a complete stranger.

The next day she set out for Gangotri - the source of the holy Ganga river - 350 km away! She had to change a number of buses - and finally ended up at Uttarkashi for the night - 115 km from Gangotri. The next day she got a bus to Gangotri - but the road was closed about 20 km from the destination due to a huge landslide blocking the road. 'No matter' she said - I will walk the 20 Km ! But the patron saint of idiots was looking out for her and - once she clambered over the landslide blocking the road - she got a seat on a taxi which was going to Gangotri.

But just visiting the Gangotri temple was too tame for her - so she bullied a bunch of tourists there to join her on a visit to Gaumukh - the actual point of the glacier where there is a dribble of meltwater which is supposed to be the starting point of the

Ganga. Those poor souls must have thought that they were stud travellers, having reached there so early in the season - but they must have changed their tone in a hurry when Bharathi chivvied them to trek across mountains and valleys to the Glacier. They stayed overnight at the ashram of a a mystic who had taken a vow of silence, and met an Austrian woman who was ordained as a sanyasin - a female ascetic - and spoke better hindi than her, a Japanese and and a couple of Germans and they chattered together on religion and lifegyaan.

She enjoyed seeing the peaks around - Bhagirathi, Shivling etc - and they made their way back to Gangotri. There they met a mountaineer who had gone to climb Bhagirathi, but had - quite literally - fallen down on the job, and had to come back with a dislocated shoulder. He had been lying there, moaning and groaning - but as soon as he saw Bharathi, he screamed with terror and jumped upright - and the jerk of that slipped his ball back into the joint with a click!

'What happened?' they asked - and he pointed a trembling finger at her.

'SHE! SHE!' he gibbered 'She had come for rock climbing at Naini tall mountaineering club 15 years ago! We survivors still remember her! EEEEEK! RUN! RUN! FOR YOUR LIVES!' and ran away, clutching his shoulder.

Everyone looked at her, and she just shrugged. Was this the face that launched a thousand rockfalls?

Then she made her way back to Uttarkashi - which was old familiar ground to her, as it was the site of her alma mater - the Nehru Institute of Mountaineering. Then she had a small trip to Dehradun and then back to

Delhi.

She wrote extensive mails about her travels and I used to wait for them and devour them greedily as they provided a window of adventure in my extremely boring working life. I was so busy - but doing nothing worth living.

One day I impulsively sent her a fan mail, telling her how much I enjoyed her mails. Much to my surprise, she replied back and wrote that she was a fan of me too! She had enjoyed the mails I had written about my travels in East India (I had gone on a backpacking trip to Bengal, Sikkim, Bhutan etc) and of course, that Kumbh mela mail.

I puffed out my chest, feeling all chuffed! I had a fan! Ha.

'Where to next?' I asked

'Everest Base Camp.' She replied
'Wow! You are going to climb Mount Everest? The tallest mountain in the world?' I asked in amazement. I wouldn't put anything beyond her.

'No' she replied - probably she wanted to add - you ignorant and credulous fool - but she controlled herself. 'Not climbing Mount Everest. I am talking about trekking to Everest Base camp. It's a long time since I have done a Himalayan trek.'

'You have done Himalayan treks?' I asked, impressed.
'Of course I have done Himalayan treks!' she was stung. 'I am a trained mountaineer! I have the Basic mountaineering course and two Advanced Mountaineering courses from the HMI and NIM!'
'What is NIM?' I asked innocently. I had only heard of IIM.

'National Institute of Mountaineering, Uttarkashi.' she replied patronisingly. 'and HMI is Himalayan Mountaineering Institute, Darjeeling.'

'Oh? It's a shame it isn't called Hmalayan Institute of Mountaineering.' I replied

'Eh? Why?'

'Then you could say that you have been to HIM and NIM. hehehehe....'

An icy blast hit me right through the email server.

'We should meet sometime.' I said casually, safe in the knowledge that she was thousands of kilometers away. 'And we can discuss trekking. I am also an experienced trekker!'

But her answer floored me!

'OK, that's a good idea. I am coming to Bombay in a few days and we will meet.'

SHIT! SHIT! SHIT! I had thought she was still in the middle of the Himalayas!
'Er….um….er….actually I am very busy….lots of work...brand relaunch and all...I can't leave the office! Yes! That's it! I just can't leave the office! Office! Can't leave! Very busy!' I babbled

But SHE was inexorable! 'That's all right. I am coming to that side of town to meet the Swiss embassy. I will meet you in your office.'

I was stunned. Blindsided. Gobsmacked.

I said the only thing I could.

'Er...OK…'

I was all aflutter as the day came for her

visit. I didn't even know what she looked like! This was before the emergence of snoop heaven, before Facebook and LinkedIn and Instagram and whatnot made it easy to find out everything about everybody.

All I knew about her was her writing and I remembered Tiwary going pale and sweating at the thought of her.

'Bah!' I thought. 'Tiwary is a spineless worm. A poltroon. A wet sock. A droopy willie. How scary can she be?'

But my imagination slowly went haywire as I started imagining someone looking like an Amazon on steroids. (no...not amazon.com silly! the Amazon women warriors!) Thoughts of Xena the warrior princess, or Wonder Woman's band of killers flashed across my mind, and I gulped. I imagined a giantess - at least 7 feet tall - with a flaming sword or something.

The moment arrived! My Nokia 1100 rang! it was SHE! I gulped and shivered!
'I am outside your office'
'I am coming out' I replied, and flexed my muscles and went down.

I looked up and down the street, looking for a termagant, an amazon, a giantess, a vampire-killer with a bloody sword...but there was no one there!

There was only one tiny little girl there, whom I passed over. She looked like a schoolgirl wearing her mom's saree for a school program or something, and i wondered who had left this foundling here, when there was no school around for miles.

I looked here and there - the street was a sausage fest! The only woman - female -

there was this little girl. But then I met her eye, and it knocked me backwards! This half-pint had the cold eye of the amazon I had expected - and being crammed into this half-portion, the power seemed to be even more concentrated!

Her eye hit me like a raw fish in the middle of the eyebrows, and left me disoriented. I was reminded of P G Wodehouse's maxim about these tiny girls - they are dashed dominating! Give them a millimetre and they take a mile, and soon you are nothing but a dashed serf!'

'Surf?'

'Serf! sort of slave!'

'Bharathi?' I asked, and she smiled and grabbed my hand. It was like being bitten by a small barracuda!

'Won't you come up?' I asked weakly.

Balsara had a pretty shitty office at the time, and I could see her eyes go wide at the sight of the entry way up. The main entrance was closed for renovation and so the entry to the marketing department was through a most shady looking staircase. It looked quite ancient - dark and shady and with an ancient winding wooden stairwell, like something that D'Artangnan would have duelled in with his peepee...er...epee. It looked as if it should have had the words 'Abandon all hope ye who enter here' emblazoned over the entrance. Ancient electrical wires hung askew like hungry pythons hunting for prey, and the ancient dusty switchboard looked like the control panel for an abandoned electric chair - haunted by the hungry ghosts of all the people it had fried to a crisp! 'Touch me, I dare you!' it seemed to say. 'I double-dare you! I triple-dare you! KHRRRR KHRRR. The building boasted a lift - but it was made in the middle-ages and was never serviced or repaired as far as I knew. It rattled and groaned asthmatically up and down like the blind dragon in Gringotts bank, and seemed to be something out of the Bates motel. I could just imagine a crazed old biddy of a secretary staggering out of it and stabbing me with a fountain pen. I never dared to use it.

We ascended the stairs accompanied by creaks and groans (by the stairs, not me. I was still young then) and entered the chamber of horrors - my office. The brand managers and other scum sat at desks which were old when Atlantis fell, and in my glory as a Marketing Manager, I rated an enclosed cubicle - about the same dimensions as a toilet stall. I cursed as a vicious nail tore a rent in my pants, and hurriedly cleared samples of air sprays and toilet cleaners from a chair and invited her to sit. She looked at the chair with suspicion and sat gingerly on it.

I looked at her again and wondered anew. Was this the brave and fearless traveller I had been reading about? I was expecting a Knight errant in shining armour. She looked like an escapee from reform school.

She also must have been looking me over - and creaming in her seat. Oooh - what a handsome virile male! she must have thought! How lordly and regal he looks sitting behind this desk. How royally he sets aside the cans and product mock-ups and how powerfully he ...er... I flailed around trying to think of complimentary things she must have been thinking about me.

We chatted a bit and she told me about her travels and adventures and about her next plans. She was going to Switzerland -

ostensibly to attend an interview at the University of Lausanne where she had applied for a second MBA. But I soon realised that this was just a convenient excuse to get a Visa while she was unemployed - she was going to explore all the Europe she could afford, and the admit would be a pleasant bonus if it happened.

I had never met anyone quite like her. She was an engineer and an MBA, and had worked in leading corporates - but she was utterly unmaterialistic. She lived for adventure travel, and a corporate job was just the most convenient and lucrative way to fund her travel.

The whole idea of a 'Sabbatical' - voluntary unemployment to travel and study - was unknown to me. I mean - all the hard work we had done all our life...school, hard work, cramming, giving competitive exams and more studying, accumulation of degrees and all that - was to get a good job and make money! Money, power, position - that was what all the struggle of life was about! All the people I knew were engaged in the accumulation of money, and clawing their way up the corporate ladder so that they could make even more money.

But no one ever thought about why they are making all that money!

'Buy a house, buy a car, nice clothes, good food and drink ...' would be the reasons one would trot out. But if you go deeper and ask WHY you want the house and the car and all the bits and bobs - they would give a blank look. Obviously the payoff of having all these goodies should be to make you happy! BUT If possessing this stuff doesn't make you happy and just makes you want more and more...then there was something wrong with the picture.

Bharathi was the first person I had met who identified what made her happy, and was pursuing it with dedication.

What a weirdo!

One great advantage of the unemployment being voluntary, rather than being the recipient of a swift kick in the pants and a pink slip - was of course that she had been able to plan the whole thing well. She had worked out a broad plan of all the places she wanted to go to, and had worked out the costs involved - and saved for it. She had disposed of all her worldly possessions - either sold them or stored them somewhere and was literally 'Of no fixed address'. She anyway was of a fairly ascetic disposition - she neither drank nor did she smoke (except when she breathed fire as a dragon) and her needs were few. EMIs and sundry fixed expenses were planned for and a contingency fund was created.

She had created a broad calendar - these months South East Asia, these months India, these months Europe, etc etc.

I didn't know what I was doing this weekend! And this one had plans for where she was going to be 6 months from next Tuesday!

'I plan to do the Everest Base camp trek after 4 months and 3 days!' she announced. 'What are your plans on that day?'

'4 months and 3 days....er ...I don't know.' I quavered.
'You don't!' she was astounded. 'Don't you have a holiday calendar planned?'
'A holiday calendar?'
'Yes! Of course! Don't you study the

calendar of the year as soon as it is released to find out when the holidays are, so that you can take advantage of long weekends and contiguous holidays?!'

'Er...no...' I said weakly

'What! Don't you book train tickets 3 months in advance just in case you get leave?'

'Er...no...'

'You mean you don't have a wishlist of holiday destinations and tentative bank of itineraries filed away?'

'Er...no...'

'You don't have a list of grandfathers, grandfathers, grand-uncles and other sundry oldies you can kill off to claim leaves?'

'Er...no...'

'You don't have a panel of doctors who can give you false medical certificates to claim spurious sick leave?'

'Er...no...'

'At least tell me that you have some

bloodstained clothes and bandages at home so that you can claim that you were in an accident?'

'Er...no...'

She leaned back in the seat and looked at me speculatively.

'Hmmm...I can see that I will have a lot of work with you.' she mused to herself.

'What?!!'

'Oh nothing, nothing...' she said dismissively 'Tell you what...let me see what happens with this Visa. We will plan the EBC trek accordingly.'

"What?!!' I jumped. 'We are? No no no no ...'

'Don't worry about it.' She said soothingly. 'See you later.'

She left, and I sat there, twitching with excitement and confusion.

What had just happened?

**The first trek**


TRING TRING TRING TRING
TRING TRING TRING TRING
TRING TRING TRING TRING

My consciousness floated up from a sea of alcohol and looked around blearily. What was that blasted noise?

TRING TRING TRING TRING

Oh it was the damn phone

TRING TRING TRING TRING

Oh all right… I am coming. I tried to stretch out my arm to pick the phone and had to think a bit to fire the correct neurons to move my arm

TRING TRING TRING TRING

I focussed my eyes with some difficulty to see who was calling - it was an unknown number. I sighed. This better not be some salesman calling to sell me credit cards or timeshare holidays. God couldn't be so cruel to a guy with a massive hangover.

'ello?' I croaked into the phone, and my head nearly exploded as a tigerish voice screamed at me
'UTHO REY! UTHO REY! UTHO REY!

'AAAAARRRGHHH' I screamed as agony shot through me as her voice fell on my throbbing brain like a hammer on a crystal vase. The voice continued mercilessly

'UTHO REY! UTHO REY! UTHO REY! UP AND AT THEM!
YOU LAZY SWINE!
GET UP!
GET UP!
GET!
UP!
GET!
UP!'

'who? what? where? when? how? why?...' I mumbled piteously. 'who is screaming...I mean...who is speaking?'

'THIS IS BHARATHI!'
'Oh'
'WE HAD DECIDED TO GO ON A TREK

TODAY!'

'Ah'

'WE WERE TO MEET AT 6 AM!'

'Oh'

'IT IS NOW 11 AM!'

'Ah'

'I HAVE BEEN CALLING FOR HOURS!'

'Oh'

'UTHO REY! GET UP! GET OUT OF BED AND GET YOUR ASS HERE!'

'Eh? here where?'

'AT THE RAILWAY STATION OF COURSE! I HAVE BEEN WAITING HERE FOR HOURS!'

'Railway? station? now?' I groaned 'But I was at my brand launch party yesterday and was drinking till 4 AM...I am in no shape to go anywhere…'

'UTHO REY AND GET OVER HERE!' She screamed with such authority, that not only me but the entire population of Chembur was at the railway station promptly, shivering with fear and sweating bullets. I had to fight my way through a huge crowd of confused and shivering people to face a grim-looking Bharathi and give her a scared grin.

'You drank all night and lowered yourself to the level of swine last night didn't you?' she demanded with ominous calm.

'I...er....'

'I can see that I will have a lot of work with you.' she mused to herself.

'Eh? What?' I asked, greatly alarmed

'Oh nothing...don't worry about it...let's get moving…'

We had planned to go trekking to a mountain fort called Harishchandragad.

The Sahyadris are a mountain range which run parallel to the Arabian sea coast and separates it from the Deccan plateau - the heartland of India. These are tough basaltic mountains - the remains of a whole buttload of ancient volcanos which blazed all over subcontinental India and created the entire Deccan plateau even before the then island of India crashed into Asia to throw up the ripples of the Himalayas. Thus these mountains are far older than the Himalayas and are craggy and pointy and have a plethora of peaks and valleys and stuff which provide ideal venues for forts, and the tough basaltic rocks provide ideal building material - the very bones of the earth itself. Add to that the fact that all trade between the coast and the heartland had to pass through a limited number of passes through these mountains which were otherwise impassable, being thickly forested with very dense and prickly trees, plants and cactus (cactuses? cactii? cactopi?). Thus it is no surprise that various dynasties over the centuries constructed forts and watchtowers all over the place, guarding these paths and passes. It must have started with mud and wood forts, which were in due course upgraded to stone forts, and later to finely engineered and artistically built ones. Most of them were built by the medieval dynasties of the Rashtrakutas and Yadavas.

Shivaji, the great Maratha king, was born and brought up in this area and used this geography to mount a highly succesful guerilla war against the various local rulers.. the various Bahamani sultans, the Mughal empire, the Siddi of Janjira etc ...and carved out the last indigenous kingdom, which later became the Maratha empire - the last great Indian kingdom before the advent of the British empire.

He made use of all these ancient forts - he upgraded some and built a few - and today they are all known in the common parlance as 'Shivaji forts'. These forts later became irrelevant with the advent of sophisticated artillery and ammunition and the 'Pax Brittanica' which put an end to local wars, and new roads and railways made the mountain passes obsolete...so they are of no use now and lie vacant and empty in the mountains, dreaming of days when greedy kings fought over them with bright swords, and created kingdoms and empires.

But they are still extremely popular with one group of people - trekkers! The Sahyadris are hot as hell in the blistering summer months, and the rocks absorb the suns heat and heat up like an oven. But, in the rains, the place really becomes a wonderland. All the pent-up life of the patient plants gushes out in the life-giving rains, and grasses and flowers spring up like magic. The mountains block the path of the rain-bearing clouds coming from the sea, causing them to let loose all the water they are carrying. The rains here are incredible to see - an experience like no other! The fierce rains, the cool winds and the incredibly vibrant 'Sahyadri green' of the fresh foliage makes this a real heaven for trekkers. All the wild flowers bloom, all the insects buzz and the wild birds sing their mating calls. There is a magic wonderland here for those who are brave enough and hardy enough to climb up these mountains.

They are a goodish way away from the city though...you have to take a local suburban train to its last stop, and then take a State Transport bus to its rural destination and then make your way to the base of the mountain - and then start climbing from there!

I started sobering up in the train journey, and listened to Bharathi talk about her expeditions. I had been reading about them in her emails, but to hear her speaking about them herself was another experience altogether - like hearing Jesus speak himself, instead of reading the Bible.

After meeting me, she had gone off to Switzerland! The ostensible reason was to give an admission interview in the University of Lausanne for a second MBA - but the only reason that she was giving the interview was to get a visa, as a jobless young hobo was not likely to be granted entry to the country.

She landed in Swissland, much to the consternation of the Switzers and bought a Swiss Rail pass and decided to take full advantage of that overpriced train ticket and explore the bloody country from cheese to bank vault. She had come here dreaming of the Swiss Alps, but decided to see the flat(ter) South as well - since the Rail Pass was anyway paid for. She travelled across the country like a head-cut chicken (a strange Indian turn of phrase. It may not be grammatically on-point, but is strangely compelling) and saw Bern, Lugano, Chur, Geneva etc in the South, and then went off to see the Swiss Riviera and the Alps - the Matterhorn area - Zermatt, Gornergrat etc, and sniffed that the Swiss need not get too high and mighty about their country - there are equally beautiful places in India. The only difference is that you have take a train, 2 buses, 3 jeeps and walk for 2 days to get there, while in Switzerland you can go there in a comfy Mont Blanc express.

From the Matterhorn area, she went to the Jungfrau area and and went and stayed in a town called Grindelwald. (I think that J K Rowling must have heard tales of a terrifying and fantastic dark person in a Grindelwald Youth hostel, and then went - A ha! - And thought of a 'dark' wizard and named him 'Grindelwald' - and wrote a book about 'Fantastic Beasts')

A fellow traveller told her about the fantastic views from Schilthorn - and she was armed with a Swiss Rail Pass, so she went there fearlessly and was struck dumb by the beauty of the views from there. The cable car climbed 3000 meters in 4 stages and at the summit, she was looking at a 360 degree Alpine panorama with Eiger, Monch and Jungfrau towering across the valley. There are about 150 peaks identified and listed in the terrace and the list includes Mt Titlis and Mt Blanc.

Rather suitably, she had a bite at the rooftop restaurant modelled after a James Bond villains lair - Pir gloria - and was shocked at the amount of Gujarati people there. Switzerland has been identified as a romance destination in India due to the sheer amount of Bollywood films being shot there, and it has become the default honeymoon destination for the moneybags

Indians. The Witless at Mt Titlis.

Bharathi gazed in horror at the giant menu of Indian food available there - basmati rice, Madras lentils, Jaipuri vegetables, papad and pickle…a sureshot indication of the number of Gujaratis visiting this place - and immediately went and ordered beef and pork, just to piss them off.

She spent a few more days travelling around Swizzland - Titlis, Lugano, Chur, Montreux etc, leaving a shoal of shocked and scared tourists, youth hostel operators and sweetz people in her wake and finally wound her European sojourn and came back to India, shouting 'I SHALL RETURN' … and the Swiss pleading 'PLEASE NO, PLEASE NO…'

Once she was back in Bombay, she said - bloody hell, this place is a sweltering dump -

and immediately flew off to the Himalayas. For someone born and raised in the equatorial flatlands of South India in Tamil Nadu, she had a very strange and ineffable affinity for the high mountains.

This time her plan was to do Lahul and Spiti region and end up in Leh, Ladakh - by bus. The journey was to take her on the Shimla - Rampur – Recong Peo - Puh - Sumdo - Tabo - Kaza - Kunzum Pass - Manali - Keylong - Leh circuit.   It turned out to be a fabulous  1500km route with mind-blowing scenery and arse-breaking roads. She saw a masked dance ceremony at Tabo monastery - where the monks put on terrifying masks representing ghosts and demons and perform complicated dances. There was a competition, and Bharathi won the award for most terrifying face - even without wearing a mask!

She took a break from the punishing rattle-bus travel by taking a break at Manali - and filled up on good food like a camel, and took a soak in the hot springs at Vashisht to sort out the kinks in her aching body. Then it was back on the roads to cross Rohtang pass and do the long ride to Leh. After spending some time in Leh, she caught a flight from Leh to Delhi and screamed in shock once she came out of the plane and the heat of Delhi hit her - it was like abruptly transiting from Siberia to Sahara!

And now she was here - in Bombay. With me!

I grew more and more uneasy as I listened to this. All I had done in my life so far was to go to East India and the Kumbh mela, and get drunk in a variety of places. I seemed to have caught a tiger by the tail!

The topic turned to trekking, and feeling that

I should also make a contribution to all this talk of adventure, I said 'I love trekking too!' Her eyes lit up! But with competitive spirit! This was her element.

'Which is your favorite trek?' she demanded 'Which all forts have you been to?'

'Er… I...er…' I opened and closed my mouth like a puzzled fish, as she looked at me challengingly. 'Er...I...um…'

'Have you been to Peb? Mangi? Tungi? Raigad? Prachandagad? Rajgad?'

'I...er….no...not quite.' I said. I had not even heard of them.

'Oh? You prefer Macchindragad? Pratapgad? Torna?'

'Er…um…' I was sweating and wilting.

'Maybe you prefer the lake view ones in the Maval?'

'er...possibly…' Silence seemed to be the best option here.

'Which ones? Tikona? Ratangad? Ballalgad?'

'Er...'

'Its fun to do just the trekking peaks, but don't you think that the technical peaks are more challenging? Putting a fixed rope and using cleats and crampons?'

'Er....sure...I suppose...'

'Or perhaps a bit of rock climbing? Like at Nanacha angtha?'

'Um...er....wow! Look at that! What... er....scenery...what...um...railway tracks!' I shouted and pointed out of the window to try and change the subject. But she was like a bloodhound on a trail, and paid me no attention.

'So how many treks have you done?' she asked a direct question, and I could prevaricate no longer.

'Er...three actually...' I mumbled

She waited for a beat, as if waiting for me to add a 'hundred' or possibly a 'thousand' to that number, and when I did not, she looked at me incredulously.

'Three? That's it? Three treks? But you told me that you were part of the trekking association in college.'

'Er...yes...but they organised one trek a year...three years, three treks.'

She rolled her eyes at me. 'What kind of Maharashtrian are you? You all keep saying 'Shivaji, Shivaji' and have never been to any of his forts.'

I shrivelled up even more, like a snail which has had salt poured on it.

It seemed that when she was working in Bombay, she used to go to the long-distance bus stand every friday night and sit in any random bus which was about to leave. Then she would ask the most puzzled conductor where the bus was going and book a ticket for the last point.Then she would take out her trekking bible - a book called 'Trek the Sahyadris' by Harish Kapadia - and see which fort was closest to that place - and go trekking there! By doing this, she had been to an awful lot of forts in the Sahyadris!

I was wide-eyed and open-mouthed when I heard this. What a crazy story! What a crazy person!
'What did you do on weekends?' she asked me.
'Er...I went ...to a pub ...or to a movie…' I replied haltingly, and she sneered at me.
'Hah. Useless fellow. Wastrel. Wimp.'

I gawped like a moron for a bit and wondered what I should do to reclaim my manhood. I flexed my muscles thoughtfully...I had been hitting the gym and was proud of my biceps. While I couldn't challenge this titch of a girl to arm-wrestle, I could show off a bit!
I grabbed hold of an overhead bar and did a pull-up, to show off my awesome muscles. I

was fully expecting her to go wide eyed and say 'Wow! You are so strong! So virile! So handsome!'

What I did not expect was for her to jump up and say 'Let's have a pull-up competition!'

'Say what?'

'It's been a long time since I did any pull-ups! Come, let's see who can do more!'

'Say what?'

She jumped up to grab the bar and quickly did 10 pull ups! I watched in horror.

'Your turn now!' she said brightly. 'Let's keep doing sets of ten. Let's see how many sets we can do!'

I went red and green and purple. Alas...I could do only one single pull-up...and I already done it. Now I would be sore for days.

'You prefer to do a push-up contest instead?' she asked eagerly. 'Or sit-ups? I tell you what...let's have a plank-off! How long can you hold your plank?'

I turned my face to the wall.

After listening to a rather tactless Sikkimese telling me bluntly that I was fat fat fat, really too fat…I had taken it to heart and had embarked on a spirited weight-loss project. I gave up booze and embarked on a strict diet and started running and hitting the gym and whatnot and had lost a bunch of weight and had become ripped and muscular. Or so I thought. But compared to Bharathi I was an invertebrate. A slug. I sighed and … you got it…I shrivelled.

We reached the last station and took an ST bus into the boondocks, and finally we were at the base of the mountain.

I looked at the huge mountain and the massing clouds. I looked at my watch  - it was nearly 4 PM!

'Shit! It is so late' I said. 'It's too late to start climbing this now!'

'Why?'

'What do you mean why?' I said with panic. 'It's already so late! It will be dark when we are halfway up the mountain! It must be a 5 hour trek up!'

'So?'

'So...so...it will be dark...on the mountain...in the rain...no light...no shelter...no change of clothes...no food…'

'Tchah!' she just waved her hand dismissively. 'That's the whole adventure! We will reach the mountain top in time to see the sunrise, and then come down for lunch. Sounds perfect.'

'But …but…' I spluttered.

'Oh come on! Are you a man or a mouse? Bloody wimp!'

I put my hands down helplessly.

I was so screwed.

My stomach rumbled, and I suddenly realised that I had not eaten anything at all today! Shit! I had to eat something - this looked like hours of climbing and no dinner either - and even breakfast would be an iffy thing.

Luckily there was a little rude stall at the start of the trail where some enterprising villager sold food and drink to trekkers. He was just winding up for the day, and happily made some hot snacks and tea for us.
'So how was the trek?' he asked, obviously assuming that we were coming down, rather than going up.
'Oh we haven't done it yet' I mumbled, scarfing down that food with 'oohs' and 'aahs' … 'we will be starting now.'
'Eh?' he looked at us, startled... then at the impending sunset, and at the massing angry

clouds. 'Another search party tomorrow...wonder what the cadaver rates are nowadays…' he mused.

'Eh? What?' I asked, jumping a foot. 'Cadaver rates?'

'Nothing...nothing…' he said soothingly. 'Do have some more food. On the house! hehehe' he said, gazing at me as if to make an estimate of my weight and height and wondering what shape my liver and kidneys must be in.

I looked at him coldly and said 'My companion is a certified mountaineer from HMI and NIM.'

'Companion? Who? Where?' he said, looking left and right. Then he looked down and noticed Bharathi glaring at him, and quailed.

'Oh! IT!'

'It?'

'HER!'

'Her?'

'SHE! SHE! SHE WHO MUST BE OBEYED! AAAAAAAAARRRGHHHH! RUN! RUN FOR YOUR LIVES!' he abandoned his stall and ran away, waving his arms about.

I looked at the figure vanishing in the distance, nonplussed.

'I came here for a trek some years back' Bharathi explained, after a while.
'Oh? Ah!'

It was darkling by the time we set out to conquer Harishchandragad, and by the time we reached about halfway, it became dark. And when I say 'dark', I mean 'DARK'. Or should I say…
DAAAAAAARRRRRKKKKKKKK…. (In a most creepy voice)

It was absolutely Stygian darkness! The clouds were so thick that not a ray of moonlight or starlight could get through. And obviously the place was an absolute wilderness, so there were no lights of any kind around. I couldn't see my hand when I held it in front of my face!

And it was raining. Hard. You ain't seen rain until you see the torrential monsoon rains in the hills. It's like a solid wall of water! But it is not freezing cold like in the Himalayas...you won't die of hypothermia out here - you will just swear a lot and shiver and feel miserable, but you wont die of it. You will just wish you were dead.

There was no help for it - we had to stop where we were. Not in any sheltered place or anything - just right there on the path. It was too dangerous to walk another step - it was like being totally blind.

We sat down in the mud and waited for the

rains to stop or the clouds to allow some light to seep through - but it didn't. It just came bucketing down and soaked us to the skin and beyond. It seemed to seep into my very bones. Then the fierce winds would dance about and take away all our body heat, and make us gasp.

I sat there musing on the vagaries of fate. Yesterday night I was at a 5 star hotel, replete with the finest booze and grub that the company budget could buy, and dancing and carousing. Today night I was sitting on a wild mountainside in absolute darkness, in a puddle of mud, next to a mad person and with the rains trying to wash us off the mountain. I was cold and hungry and damp.

Not that I was sad about it...I was enjoying an off-the-cuff adventure after a long time, and loved the splendid variety in my life.

We huddled closer and closer in that dark rainy night, and finally ended up cuddling...to share body heat of course. Hypothermia is dangerous. You could die of it. Cuddling…warm…soft…cuddle in the puddle…mmm

Ahem. (Clears throat)

We had to sit there all night, and I sighed when finally the pale streaks of pre-dawn light came up and lighted up our world. That darkness had really been something.

We scampered up the mountain, and I shuddered as we crossed some very steep and slippery passes and narrow mountain gaps. It was a very good thing we stopped where we did. It would have been a sure-shot suicide to have tried it in the dark. As I passed it, I thought I heard a villager say

'Oh shit. Bad luck. They survived.'

I thought it was a really tough trek. It was steep and slippery and replete with broken stairways and narrow paths and I was gasping and covered with mud as we finally reached the top. But I was extremely happy with myself! All that jogging and gymming and dieting had actually paid off! I was a machine! I had conquered this amazingly difficult climb up the mountain with style, inspite of the long boozy night the night before, the long rainy night, and no food. I was the man!

I looked at her proudly, waiting for the oohs and aahs of admiration for my feats.

And Bharathi says 'Actually I think this fort is too easy. Next time I will take you on something more challenging. This is no fun.'

I glared at her in disbelief, but she totally ignored me. Or couldn't see my face as it was totally covered in mud.

The top of the fort was still covered in mist and clouds and visibility was hardly 20 paces or so. We scared the shit out of a trekker who had spent the night comfortably in a barn, and was just coming out to see the dawn, yawning and scratching his balls. He yammered at the sight of two mud covered people suddenly emerging out of the clouds and walking towards him in a threatening manner.

'EEEK! GOLEMS! DEMONS!' he screamed and ran away, waving his arms.

I jumped up in alarm, but Bharathi was totally unmoved. She seemed to be used to people seeing her and running away in terror.

Harishchandragad was a very ancient fort, built by the Yadavas or Rashtrakutas or some such ancient dynasts. The very name of the fort referred to King Harishchandra - the dude who had been mentally so screwed by a sage. H was supposed to be a total boy scout - one of the dudes who keep their word, no matter how stupid it is. The sage asked for a boon - but he would not say what the boon was unless the king agreed to fulfill it, whatever it may be.

'Only if you agree to that are you truly royal.' the sage sneered at him 'Else you are just a trader!'

Instead of kicking the bearded dude up the butt, H agreed to the pig-in-the-poke demand, and his flabber was totally gasted when the sage then demanded his entire possessions - his crown, his kingdom and even his pants!

'What!' H said, slapping his brow 'I thought you will ask for a sack of rice and some gold or something!'

'NO NO NO...no backsies. You totally promised! So hand me the keys and your pants and get moving!'

Instead of calling his soldiers and getting el beardo thrown out of the palace, good-boy-H meekly handed over everything and walked out of his kingdom, pantless.

Then all kinds of mayhem happened - he and his family were sold as slaves - his wife and kid went somewhere and he himself was sold to the king of the corpse-burners - the guys who burn dead bodies at the ghats...the lowest of the low, so to speak.

Then to add the cherry on the top, one day his wife turns up at the ghat bearing the body of her dead son! She begs good-boy-H to burn the kid, but he says that he is the servant of his master and cannot burn bodies without payment.

'Alas! I have nothing.' the ex-queen sobs, probably wondering why she married this

loser in the first place. 'I am a slave. I have no possessions.'
'Then hand me your clothes' he demands, revealing a rather kinky side to his personality.

But before she can actually strip naked, the sage appears like a wizard high on floo-powder and says NONONO… keep those clothes on...everybody relax. Then he snaps his fingers and hey presto - they are back in their palace. The whole thing had been an illusion created by the sage to test whether H was much of a boy scout as he claimed! All hail king H, the noblest person around.

This is a great legend in India and every good and truthful person is referred to as 'a regular Harishchandra'. I never thought much of this weird story myself - a king who agrees to hand over his responsibilities to some random dude cannot be considered a good ruler. What would el beardo know about administration and ruling? What would happen to the population? Wouldn't the neighbouring king lick his lips and attack such a demoralised kingdom right away?

Wouldn't this disgusting example ensure that people think that keeping one's word is a stupid idea, and one should never ever do it?

I shrugged my shoulders. Legends are strange.

The fort itself was totally awesome, like all Sahyadri forts. It was built out of gigantic stone blocks, and cunningly designed for offense and defense. Those ancient fort builders were really something. To create this huge thing on top of a steep mountain, with no modern technology - a mind-boggling feat. And we have so many of such forts that we don't even give them a second glance.

Unfortunately, because it was so cloudy, we couldn't see any views - which was a pity because the views were supposed to be awesome. There was a spot called the 'konkankada' where - apart from watching views - convicted criminals would be thrown off the cliff to land with a splat below! This was called 'kadelot' and was a vicious form of capital punishment.

We looked around, saw nothing, and decided to get some breakfast.
'There is a cave right about there..' Bharathi pointed 'A villager makes breakfast and tea for trekkers there.'
'Oh? Have you been here before?'
'Yes...I must have come here about 10 years back.'
I looked at her with respect. I can barely

remember where the toilet in my office is. My memory is that inspired type where I can get lost in my own home. If the cops ever suspect me of a crime and ask me 'Where were you on the morning of so and so date?', I would just put my hands forward for them to slap on the handcuffs. And she can remember a tea-serving cave from a decade ago!

We found that cave and entered it - and it was like entering the domain of a shaman or witchdoctor! The place was dark and filled with swirling smoke, and a one-handed man with wild hair and glittering eyes was squatting in front of a fire. He looked like a necromancer about to do a human sacrifice, and I half-expected him to lift up a skull and shout ALAKH NIRANJAN and throw human ashes about, or prance about a cauldron and welcome me with 'All hail MacBeth, thou shalt be king hereafter' or something.

'Welcome! I was waiting for you!' he said in a spine-chilling voice, which ...er...chilled my spine.
'W-W-W-waiting for us?' Why? What for?' I quavered. He must have a vision of us climbing up, and had decided that we would the perfect human sacrifice or something.
'For breakfast of course' he said, brandishing a knife at us.
Oh shit! He was going to eat us for breakfast! He was a cannibal as well as a witchdoctor! A witchibal. A cannidoctor!
''For b-b-b-breakfast?'
'Yes. Didn't you guys order breakfast and tea? The poha is almost ready.'
'Eh?' My vision suddenly cleared, and it turned out that the guy was just a cook with bad hair. The fire was not a mystic apparatus, but just a cooking arrangement. And smoke was just ...well, smoke from the

cooking fire.And his eyes were glittering because he was high on grass.

'Oh...ah! No no...We weren't the ones who ordered the breakfast, but we have come to have some. Breakfast. We have come for ...er...breakfast.' I babbled, still a bit shaken.

One-handed-sam handed us two steaming platefuls and we tucked into them gratefully. He was bit surprised to see fresh trekkers so early in the morning - normally the people who have breakfast are the ones who have stayed overnight. The people who start trekking in the morning reach up there for lunch. We told him our story and he shook his head at us. But he was high on grass so he kept on nodding for a long time before he stopped.

'I recognise you.' He suddenly said, looking at Bharathi. 'Weren't you here 10 years ago.'

'Yes I was.' She said proud that she was so memorable that even this marijuana smoker remembered her after such a long time.

'And this is a new one, eh?' he said, pointing his stump at me.

'Eh?' I said, with a start. 'What was that?'

'Nothing nothing…' they both said in unison. 'Eat your breakfast.'

The walk down had none of the drama of the climb and we were soon down to the base and then did the whole journey in reverse - bus and train back to Bombay.

As we said goodbye, Bharathi looked at me speculatively and muttered 'I think he will do…'

'What was that?'

'Nothing nothing...bye. That trek was fun...I will get back to you.'

'Get back to me? On what?'

'On our dates for the Everest Base Camp trek of course.'

'Our dates?!' I looked at her in shock 'For Everest...what?'

'Never mind...don't worry about it. I will send you your orders.'

'What? Orders? For what?' I said alarmed

'Oktatabye' she said, walking off.

'But...but…What did you mean by Everest base camp? You mean Everest…the Everest? The highest mountain in the world? But I am knackered just by Harishchandragad! Hey…hey…'

But I was just talking into the wind. SHE had vanished.

**Off to Nepal**

'Chalo bye dad' I said, shouldering my bag.
'I am off to the Everest base camp'
'OK bye' my dad said absently, engrossed in his newspaper.

As I closed the door, I heard the newspaper rustling to the floor and my dad saying 'Er...umm.. You are going where?!!'

When Bharathi told me that we are going to the Everest base camp, my reaction had been of total incredulity. I had never been on an overnight trek (except the lost on mountain one), much less a Himalayan trek. And here we were talking about going to the base of the highest mountain in the world! The whole idea was ridiculous! How will I be able to do it? How will I get the leave from work? How will I get permission from home? How will I afford it?

But the thing about Bharathi is that - like Steve Jobs - she generates her own personal reality distortion field! Just a chance meeting with her, and you end up doing things you never dreamt of! There are hundreds and hundreds of people who black out after meeting her, and wake up in a strange country - passport in one hand, and itinerary in the other, wandering aimlessly around with a shocked look on their faces.
All you have to do is to make a random statement 'I wish I could go to {insert country here} or do {insert random dangerous activity here}...' and the half-pint would fix them with a glittering eye and

demand 'Well, why don't you?!'

That person would reply with some logical explanation - it's too expensive / I am too old / too fat / too unfit /  etc...but she would just transfix him/her/it with a contemptuous eye and say - if you can dream it, you can do it! Get off your fat lazy butt and let's go!

But...but…

But nothing! Hand me your checkbook! And your credit card! I will do all the bookings and chalk out the itinerary.

The poor fool would feebly try to resist - but it would be of no use. He would be in her hypnotic power and be sucked in to her alternate reality.

And sure enough, everything clicked into place. My boss  - a guy who would cringe about giving you leave for any reason, and which normally had to be extracted out of him with anaesthesia and heavy machinery - just said 'Oh! Ah! Trekking? In Nepal?

OK.' Those were the days before easy internet bookings - but my cousin had just become a travel agent, and he fixed me up with tickets to Kathmandu. I had no trekking gear at all - I didn't even know there was anything called trekking gear.

This was back in 2002, and there was no Amazon and no Decathlon or any place where one could easily get good quality mountaineering gear of any sort. But I asked around and I found a shop which was owned by a former mountaineer and he sold all these knickknacks and doohickeys. I presented myself at his door, and he looked at me doubtfully.

'YOU are going to EBC? YOU? Really?' he said in wonderment.

Yes, I was - I assured him and told him that I was in the market for a nice backpack. He sold me a huge backpack - I could have packed Bharathi into it! But I thought that since I was going for month and there might not be an opportunity to wash clothes and stuff, I should carry enough clothes for a month. I shoved it full of T shirts and shorts and whatnot and it looked ready to explode!

And what else was there to do? I had sneakers, I had a backpack - I was all set! I had this rather strange philosophy that one should wear old clothes and old shoes for a trek - thus even if it gets muddy or dirty or torn during a hike it would be no great loss. And once your clothes get dirty - you just throw them out instead of washing them. Thus your pack become lighter and lighter as time goes on, and you can use that space to store memorabilia and knick-knacks in. Thus I was carrying old and throwable clothes and torn and shitty 'Power Jogger' sneakers. And a cap.

I was all set!

Or so I thought.

The day dawned finally and I proudly lifted my huge backpack with a grunt and cheerily told my folks that I was off to Nepal - the thing that caused my dad's newspaper to drop to the floor.

I took a cab to the International airport and it felt seriously weird to be there in the daytime. At that time (and even now for that matter) most international flights from India took off in the dead of the night, at the most inconvenient time possible. This was because the flights wanted to be in and out of foreign airports at a convenient time and no one cared if it inconvenienced Indians. Screw them. They would tolerate all kinds of abuse anyway.
Thus the airport would be full and buzzing in the night and would be sleepy and deserted in the daytime.

But Nepal hardly counted as an international flight - it was just there on the border. Just slightly further than Lucknow - so those flights left in the day. I was flying on the Nepalese national carrier - the most romantically named 'Royal Nepal Airlines'. I arrived happily whistling to the counter, only to be greeted by a sign - 'Flight to Kathmandu delayed by 12 hours'.

Bloody hell. So it was only scheduled to depart in the day - It would be leaving in the night after all.

I wondered what to do for 12 hours at the airport - and then decided to go back home to a most amused family and come back in the night. While in the cab, a story idea struck me…what could happen to a guy in this situation? Suppose he decides to stay in a hotel instead of going home? Suppose he meets a guy who wants to murder him? Why would the guy want to murder him? How would the murder be planned? What would be the twist?

I used to write a lot of fiction in those days and a story just came and flitted into my mind. I quickly jotted the idea down in my journal and later wrote a story called 'The second sense'. It turned out as a damn good story and later I published it in a short story collection called 'Bombay Thrillers'. (Shameless plug! Read the book!)

The trip was off to a great start! I had a story already! WooHoo!

I came back cursing and complaining in the dead of the night, and cleared the mess of immigration and customs and security and whatnot and finally boarded the Royal Nepal Airlines flight to Kathmandu at some ungodly hour in the night.

I had just dropped off to sleep when the nepali airhostess came and woke me up repeatedly to offer me booze, then dinner, then tea, and then breakfast in quick succession and ensured that I was bleary-eyed and sleep-deprived as I landed in Kathmandu.

Indians don't need a visa or even a passport to enter Nepal and so clearing immigration was a breeze.

The interesting part was the huge number of signs shouting and screaming that Rs 500 and Rs 1000 denomination INR notes are not accepted in Nepal - because the Pakistani government had printed oodles and oodles of fake Indian currency and splashed it around in Nepal. It was a win-win for Pakistan - they are able to buy all kinds of stuff and pump terrorists into India via Nepal for free, and it is India and Indian money which is treated with suspicion. It's like getting a punch in the face from a masked attacker and then being arrested for having a black eye!

But I was aware of this and had exchanged all my 500s and 1000s for 100 rupee notes and had warned Bharathi about it on email. She had replied saying that of course she knew it - she knew everything - she knew much more than I did about anything and everything and how did I dare to give her any advice, eh?

In addition to the 100 rupee notes stash, my dad also gave me a 100 USD note.
'What will I do with US dollars in Nepal?' I asked
'Keep it.' My dad said 'You never know when US dollars can come in useful'
I smirked and kept the cash just to assuage

his feelings. Little did I know how useful that was to prove later.

I made a beeline to Thamel in old Kathmandu. New Kathmandu is like any other city - only more polluted, because they adulterate their petrol with cheap kerosene from India. But old Kathmandu is awesome. It was the ancient capital of Nepal and was full of ancient temples and buildings and with a charming network of small streets and squares. It is very romantic and colourful, and the streets are full of tourists rather than busy commuters - which gives it a relaxed chilled-out vibe.

Thamel was a backpacking hotspot which was full of cheap hotels and restaurants serving firang food, and lined with colourful stalls selling tourist kitch and trekking equipment and stuff.

Bharathi would be landing in Kathmandu the next day, so I had the day to myself to explore the place.

Nepal is sort of like the skinny guy on a bus seat wedged between two large bruisers, who smell bad and hog the seat and poke you with their elbows - but you are too afraid to object. It is wedged between the two Asian giants - India and China - and is squashed a bit from both sides. Earlier they had a much more neighbourly neighbour in Tibet - like an eccentric relative or fellow villager living next to you. You have the occasional spat, but on the whole you come from the same stock and so you get along. But then Tibet was hijacked by China (that too Mao's Communist China, which had a reputation of killing millions and millions of it's own citizens on a whim, so you can just imagine what they did to conquered Tibet) and suddenly you have a scary homicidal neighbour with a lot of guns and a bad disposition. He has already killed your old neighbour and so you are shit scared of him! Nepal has to walk a fine line to avoid pissing either of its neighbours off - as it has an equally long border with both of them.

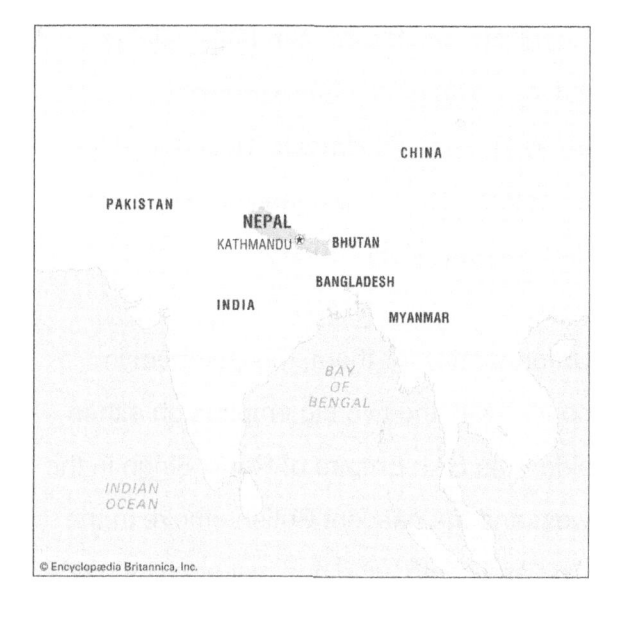

In the middle ages, Nepal used to be a loose collection of kingdoms - much like every other place in the world at that time. And like in the rest of the world, there was a movement towards crystallisation to form a large country. Various warlords conquered swathes of territory and bigger warlords swallowed smaller ones and finally in 1769, a guy called Prithvi Narayan Shah emerged on top of the heap and became king of Nepal. He and his descendants celebrated this by going on to conquer neighbouring areas in India, Sikkim and Tibet and were no doubt planning to conquer even more and become a big country.

Unfortunately for them, this put them in conflict with the two big empires on either side - the Sikh Empire of Ranjit Singh in the west and the nascent British empire in the east and south, who had just won the battle of Plassey and thus were rulers of North India and had started on their little project of conquering the whole of India.

The Nepalis fought hard and bravely, but still got their asses handed to them by both empires and had to give back all the territory they had conquered and retreat back to their borders. But the fighting skills of the Gurkhas of the Nepali army so impressed both the British and the Sikhs that they invited the Gurkha soldiers to join their own armies. The Gorkha regiments thus formed went on to become some of the most feared and respected fighting forces in the world. Even now there are Gorkha regiments in the Indian army, the British army, and even in Singapore and Brunei.

An interesting word that came out of this was the Nepali word for one who works abroad - 'Lahori'. The first guy to enroll Gorkha soldiers in his army was Emperor Ranjit Singh of Lahore. A lot of the Nepali fighting force was extremely disgruntled with their king's surrender to the British East India Company forces, and rather than serve under them, they decided to become mercenaries for the Sikhs and moved to Lahore. So many people went to Lahore, that the very word for a person who works abroad became 'Lahori'.

It was therefore deeply ironic that the majority of the forces of the East India Company in the Anglo-Sikh wars, in which the British conquered and destroyed the Sikh empire just a few years after this - were Gorkhas.

I went exploring around and saw the sights - Nepal was at the time an official Hindu kingdom (Now it is officially a secular republic) and it's most famous shrine was the the famous Pashupatinath temple by the banks of the river Bagmati. It is a grand temple complex honouring Lord Shiva as

'Pashupati' - 'the god of all living things' (not just humans), and has a cremation ghat just by the river, with a number of idiotic white tourists taking photos of the cremations. (Why would you take photos of last rites? Would you like it if a bunch of Canon-toting Japanese tourists came to your mom's funeral and did yakkety-yak and took photos of the casket being buried?)

(An interesting thing about this temple is that the priests here are traditionally 'Bhattas' from far-off Karnataka in South India. Nepali priests can only assist them, but are not allowed to actually perform rites and ceremonies. There is an ancient tradition in India of importing priests from other places - South Indian priests in North Indian temples and vice versa. This is probably to prevent local powerful people from dominating the temple. I find it really fascinating!)

Another icon of old Kathmandu is the 'Kumari' temple, which was the residence of the current 'Devi' or 'living goddess'. This is a human person - a little girl who is considered an avatar of the Goddess in human form and is worshipped as a divinity. The priests search for the right candidate from amongst hundreds - the girl should have the correct horoscope, physical characteristics and mental makeup and whatnot - and should be pre-pubescent. Once she attains puberty and menstruates, she can no longer be the Devi and has to make place for the next candidate.

It must be a pretty weird life for such a little girl - 4 to 6 years old - to be plucked from parents and family and from her life, and then be made to stay in a mouldy old palace, be made up like a doll with fancy clothes and over-the-top make up and be exhibited every day from a window for people to worship! And then be chucked out of it in a few years - by the time she is 13-14 years old. Life must be tough for ex-devis.

Nepal was full of tourists from all over the world, and as an Indian I was almost a local, but not quite. The locals could communicate with me in Hindi and talk about India and Bollywood movies and film stars - but I was obviously not Nepali. The locals seemed to be desperate to target the white tourists, and ignored me completely. I didn't mind it at all, not being the target of high-pressure sales talk and incessant questions of 'Hello friend! Where you from?' was a great treat. It seemed to be a bit of a wasted effort to me - many white backpackers are great bargainers and are as tightfisted as an oyster with lockjaw - the shopkeepers would probably have more success with me….but don't tell them that! My only defense against these guys is to give a contemptuous smirk and shake my head. If I showed the slightest interest in anything, the savvy salesmen would be emptying my pockets in no time.

While walking around, I saw a barber shop - and I had a great idea!

I would shave my head!

I always wanted to try out the baldy look, but never had the guts to actually try it out. In Indian culture, men shave their head when a close relative dies, and so it is seen as a greatly inauspicious thing to do. People would come and ask in hushed voices 'All well? What happened?' and my parents would say waspishly 'We are still alive, you know!'
But here there was no such issue. I would be stylishly bald, and my hair would grow

back a bit by the time the trek ended. I would be as handsome as Vin Diesel or Bruce Willis or whoever is the current skinhead heartthrob!

Lets go for it!

I marched into the barbershop and demanded that he shave my head.
The guy was flummoxed, but then shrugged his shoulders. Being in Thamel, he must have got used to strange requests. Probably he was disappointed that I didn't ask for something more extreme - a mohawk, or cutting hair in the shape of an 'Om' or something.
He got to work with a vengeance, snipping and cutting until it was short enough to take out his machine and lay into my hair like an enthusiastic suburban dad running his lawnmower through his lawn.
I started having doubts about my decision

when I saw that bare strip of scalp - but it was too late to do anything now. He lawnmowered my head with a hair-clipper, and then finished off by lathering up my skull and shaving it smooth with a dangerous looking cut-throat razor. All that was required was to take some wax polish and a strip of cloth and buff up my skull like a car polish!

I looked a real sight. My scalp had never actually seen the sun - it was always covered by hair - and the skin was clean and untanned. My face was tanned and brown - but was now topped by a pale white dome.

I looked like a light bulb. A dim one.

Shit. Rather than looking cool like Bruce Willis or Vin Diesel, I looked like a pale white 40W LED lightbulb, which you would use in the toilet.

My skull seemed to be entirely the wrong shape to look cool bald. I looked more like a cancer patient than a cool dude! What a disappointment.

Oh well. At least I wouldn't have to worry about combing and shampooing for a bit.

When I got back to Thamel, I suddenly realised that the head-shaving had effected a sea-change in how I looked. I was inundated by the shopkeepers. With my shiny pale dome, I must looked like a firang! I could hardly move a step without a 'Helloofraand...whereufrom...come to my shop...I give you best price…'

One shady looking guy stopped me in the street and asked me I had wanted to buy any Marijuana. I looked at him, wondering what to say! I had never been targeted by a ganja seller ever. But before I could say a word, a police van screeched to a halt behind me and made me jump! Two fat cops jumped out and yelled at the shady guy 'Hey you! What are you doing?' The shady guy was so taken by surprise that he couldn't think of a word to say, and within seconds they grabbed him and threw him into the van and drove off! The cops gave me a piercing glance which shook me to the core!

Shit!

I was rattled by the suddenness of it all. Good thing I hadn't opened any negotiations with the guy, or I might have been in that van too! My bald head had too much sex appeal apparently! It was too much power to handle! I covered it with a piece of cloth and slunk off to bed.

The next morning I went off to Kathmandu airport to meet Bharathi. It had been a long time since we had met, and I had an irrational fear that I would be able to recognise her!

But it turned out that she was the one who had the recognition problem. I saw her as she came out and smiled and waved enthusiastically - and she shrieked and jumped, and scowled and got into a combat pose! 'You bald villain! How dare you molest me? I will tear you from limb to limb! I will cut you into pieces and dance on the remains! I will cut off your head and use your skull as my drinking cup! HAI!'
'Nononono....' I said worriedly, waving my hands at her. 'It's me...Ketan!'
'What?' She looked at me closely, and then sighed. She probably had dreams of going trekking with a good-looker, and now she

would be saddled with villainous-looking baldy - who looked like one of those disposable villains, one of the guys to be casually bashed up by the hero before he takes on the main baddie.

I took her to my hotel, and she laughed as she saw my backpack. 'What is this huge thing? Are you planning to leave your job and become a sherpa out here? This is twice as big as it needs to be! Throw out half this shit at once!'

'But...but...I thought we wont have time to do laundry anywhere...so I brought fresh clothes for everyday.'

'You don't pack unlimited clothes you moron. You take limited clothes, and wash them! Remove half this stuff! This bag is also a most ridiculous bag. It is too big and too heavy.'

She told me that she had done a 3 month

backpacking trip of South East Asia with just a few grams of luggage. After our little trek which almost killed me, but was just a refreshing break for her - she happily hopped on a flight to Bangkok with just 1059 dollars, a camera and a Lonely Planet 'South East Asia on a Shoestring' and done a trip across 3 countries - Thailand, Laos and Cambodia - with nothing but a half backpack of possessions!

Why then, did I need to carry a whole truck load of crap for a trek of a few weeks, eh?

Why? Why ? Why?

She threw out half my stuff until I feared that I would have to do the trek naked! Finally there was nothing else to throw out, but she still glared and clucked and hissed. But there was nothing more to be done unless I cut off a hand or a leg or something.

Luckily she didn't have a butcher knife close to hand, so there was nothing more to be done than to start off.

The trek for the Everest base camp started from a village called Jiri. Then it was apparently a weeks walk to Lukla, where there was a tiny airport. Most people flew from Kathmandu to Lukla and back. We would be walking the whole route up, and taking the flight back from Lukla.

Bharathi told me all this, of course. I wouldn't know the difference between a Jiri and a Jedi, or a Lukla from a hoopla. You couldn't find a more ignorant guy than me. I just nodded smartly and saluted smartly and said 'Yes Ma'm' smartly. And that pretty much set the note of our relationship from then on.

Our hotel guy offered to book bus tickets from Kathmandu to Jiri, but Bharathi sneered at his asking price.
'What nonsense! He wants double the fare! We will just go to the bus stand ourselves and book tickets directly.'

The bus stand was chaotic and bewildering, like all such places in Asia, but we managed to find the correct bus and squeeze our way into it. And 'squeeze' being the important word! The bus was jam-packed with villagers going back home from the capital. They were villagers who had come to the capital to meet relatives or transact business or buy stuff from the bazaars, and the bus was full of excited women clutching bags and baskets and packages. All the seats got taken in a matter of seconds and one poor guy who had bought a seat ticket just couldn't get to his seat and bitched and complained all the way.

The most interesting part of the journey for me was the conductor. He was a cheerful smiling young guy, with the body of a kung-fu star! The bus was so packed that he couldn't walk up and down the aisle to sell tickets - so he used to climb out of a windows, move like Spiderman across the outside of the bus and climb in through the next window! While the bus was speeding and careening wildly along the twisty Himalayan roads! I looked at him wide-eyed, but no one else seemed to think it in any way unusual. And the guy never lost his smile for an instant. Incredible.

After a long and tiring journey, we finally reached Jiri and checked into a hotel. The hotel was so cheap that Bharathi got the jitters and thought that definitely someone is going to rape me and loot her in the night… er…no….the other way around. I think.

We went out for a stroll in the night, and I was entranced by that starry sky. What a sight! What a night! What stars! I was … er…starry eyed! That was magical. And that was just the start!

I was so excited.

We would start the trek tomorrow!

**The trek starts**

The next morning dawned and I shouldered my absurdly large backpack as SHE rolled her eyes at me, and we set out of the hotel.

The entry to the trail was by leaving the village through a shady looking route - it looked like the way to the outhouse and smelt of pee. I stopped for a moment and looked doubtfully at it - but Bharathi confidently walked ahead and I followed.

This was it! We were on the road! The road to Everest!

The trail instantly became a charming forest walk after we left the village behind and I was oohing and aahing at the beauty of the mountain trail. We were still in the foothills and the forests were covered with dense forests, and we went up hill and down dale as we walked to the next village. It was so beautiful! Gentle green mountains, beautiful streams and little rivers, stone paths, blue skies and birds chirping here and there.

One can think of Nepal as a layer cake.

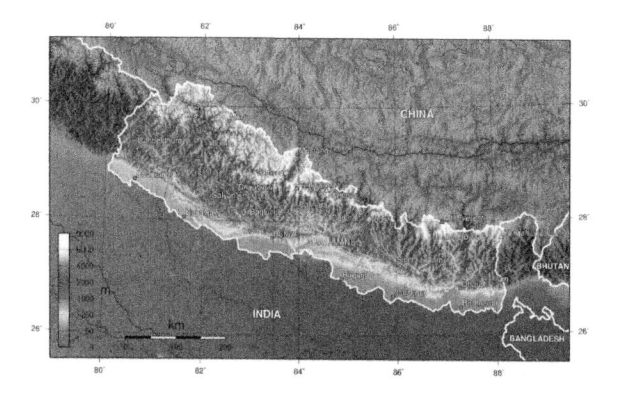

The bottom layer is the plains - the Terai region - which is quite similar to India. This is the granary of Nepal, where the bulk of the agriculture, industry and trade and most of the population is. This is the Hindu dominated area, and culturally closer to India. The next layer is the lower Himalayas. These mountains are not very high and are below the tree line, and hence are green and forested. Then comes the Tibetan plateau part - it is very high and once you cross the tree line, it becomes a high altitude desert - no trees, just a few shrubs and grasses. This area is culturally closer to Tibet and most of the inhabitants are Tibetan Buddhists. This is where you find all the great peaks - Everest and its 8000 meter+ cousins.

**Classic Route Jiri to Everest- Khumbu**

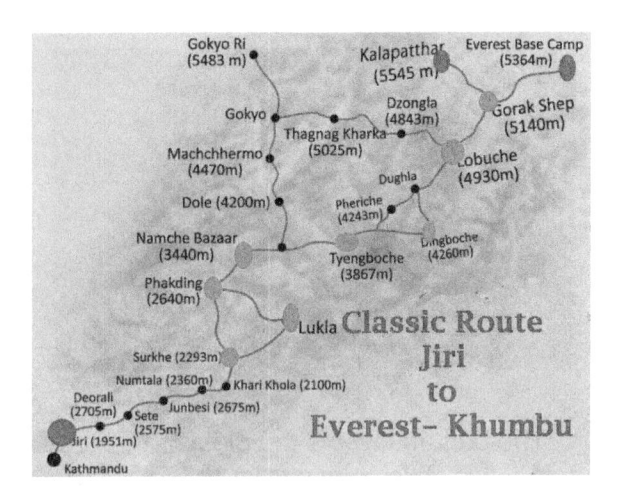

All this was ex-post-facto information to me obviously...I had no idea where we were and where we were going. I was just putting one foot in front of the other and soaking in the scenery and the sheer experience of my first ever Himalayan trek.

'How could you just go off on such a huge trek?' everyone asked me. 'No experience, no information and without knowing anything about your companion?' I did not know Bharathi much at all after all - I had just read her emails and gone on that one trek with her. I didn't even know her surname! I knew almost nothing about her.

I don't know. I just did it. I had been feeling hemmed in and encircled by life for some time and I just wanted to launch myself into life and let it take me where it willed. I closed my eyes and trusted to fate - it just seemed like the right thing to do.

I think it is very important to be flexible in life and just go with the flow. People talk about drawing up plans and goals and whatnot, and having a strategy and taking fate by the foreskin (or something like that...) - but sometimes it is even better to just lie back and ride on the river and let it take you wherever it wills. It will take you beyond your comfort zone, out of familiar haunts and to new lands and new experiences which you never dreamt of. Cast off! WooHoo!

Or maybe I am just a lazy sod.

All I knew that I was thoroughly enjoying myself.

While we trekked, Bharathi told me of her adventures on the South East Asia backpacking trip.

She had started out in Bangkok - from all she had heard from lecherous Indian tourists, she expected the place to be nothing but a gigantic and seedy strip joint - A Sodom and Gomorrah kind of place full of lust and debauchery - but she had been pleasantly surprised! Bangkok turned out to be a lovely city, full of colour and culture. She explored a number of beautiful temples - Wats - and had gone oooh and aah over the beautiful carvings and sculpture. Wat Traimit had a giant golden statue of the Buddha, made of 5 tonnes of gold! Wat Pho turned out to be a giant 20 acre temple complex with very impressive structures, chedis and Buddha statues, notably the 46meter reclining golden Buddha - which took 4 hours to explore. The temple is famous for having a Thai massage school run by monks, and she melted into a blissful puddle after getting kneaded like bread dough there.

After Bangkok, she visited the famous 'Bridge on the river Kwai' and spent the time in a WWII haze as she explored the JEATH war museum and the Allied war cemetery and hummed 'The paths of glory…lead but to the grave' and felt very proud of herself. Then she went to Pattaya and enjoyed beaching around on those splendid shores. She was obviously not interested in the whoring, and so saved a lot of money that a horny male would throw around here. She explored various beaches and temples and ancient cities and lots and lots and lots of Buddhas - standing, sitting, lying! They really loved their Buddhas. The best thing in Thailand was the food - she couldn't read the signs, so she used to randomly point at stuff and then swallow it with gay abandon. It was uniformly brilliant - as long as you avoid the insects and scorpions and stuff.

She went for a trek there too - she is incorrigible! She went to a place called Um Phang and did a jungle trek - which included river rafting and an elephant ride as well. The proprietor turned out have studied in India - and he was so thrilled at meeting a solo Indian female traveller in Um Phang, that he offered her a sweet discount on the trek. It turned out be an excellent experience - they started with a splendid session of river rafting, then soaking in a hot spring, then furious white-water rafting, then a jungle trek, stayed in a jungle lodge overnight and then went to see the giant waterfall at Thilawsu. It was the 6th largest waterfall in the world, and she had to anchor herself like Tarzan, clutching on to lianas and roots to prevent herself being washed away with the force of the water. Then she went and terrorised some tribals and took an elephant ride and so on.

Trekking in Nepal is not like trekking in other countries where you are hiking in the wilderness and you will not meet any other living soul - except other hikers. Here the trails are highways - normal roads for all traffic. There are no motorable roads and so all traffic is on foot. You see villagers going here and there on their day-to-day business, and you have porters and yaks carrying loads from place to place. All traffic is on foot, and there is no wheeled vehicle in sight.

Thus the trails are not lonely and solitary walks - you keep seeing people and villages and shops and tea-houses and such like. It was a bit disorienting for a bit, but then we got used to it and appreciated the fact that we didn't need to carry food and drink and tents and stuff - everything was available enroute. We stopped for a refreshing chai after about three hours and I congratulated myself on being a good hiker.
'This is a piece of cake!' I thought to myself. 'I rock!'

This feeling vanished almost immediately after that - because we came to the first pass of the trek- Deorali pass. It was a pretty steep pass, and I gasped and huffed and puffed as I made my way up to it. All thoughts of appreciating the scenery vanished as I grimly concentrated on climbing up that slope. GASP. WHEEZE. GASP.

The weather at passes is always

unpredictable, and it was looking black and cloudy on top of the pass. Bharathi looked at it, then looked at me and pursed her lips doubtfully.

Luckily there was a very nice guesthouse right at the pass and so we decided to stay there for the night and not push on to the next village, which had been our…er…her target for the day. The rooms were extremely reasonable and nice, and our hostess was very sweet as well, so it was a pleasant end to our first day of hiking.

I was very pleased! The first day had been a great success!

As we relaxed in the guest house, I thought about how strange that the mountain whose base we were aiming for - the place where so many thousands of trekkers and mountaineers come to every year and millions more fantasise about - is a such a recent discovery. It didn't even have a name till about a hundred years ago.

Mount Everest is named after a grumpy English surveyor - Sir George Everest, who was an army officer and ended up as the Surveyor General of India. He would be even grumpier today knowing that his name is mispronounced all over the world.

Almost everyone pronounces the name as EVER REST - with the 'ever' rhyming with 'never'; and this would have got the old beardo foaming with rage. His name was EVE - REST…like the naked lady in the garden of Eden. Just think of Eve resting after that first fuck with Adam, with the apple in her…hand? Mouth? …well…wherever she put it, and the snake sniggering away and Gabriel just about to light his sword on fire (I keep thinking of a frustrated guy with a defective cigarette lighter…click click click…damn and blast it…click click click… light, damn you…click click click…I am going to throw you in the gutter…click click click…) and there you have the correct way to say his name. EVE REST.

In the 1800s most western cartographers and mountaineers firmly believed that the highest mountains in the world were the Andes in South America. Nobody had much information about the new possessions of the British empire (well, technically of the British East India Company ) and the company decided to map out their new territories and figure out how big the place actually was.

This was an age when scientists and philosophers were beginning to appreciate the value of solid accurate information, and so they decided to rigorously and scientifically map out India. This came to be called the 'Great Trigonometric survey' or 'The great arc' and this became one of the biggest and most challenging mapping expeditions of the world.

After the EIC defeated the armies of Tipu Sultan in the Anglo-Mysore wars and became de-facto rulers of South India, they decided to do a proper and scientific mapping of the place, and appointed a guy called Major Lambton to carry out a proper trigonometric survey. This involved lugging a heavy instrument called a 'theodolite' to various high points and then taking a very accurate sighting of a flag or landmark at another high point and accurately measuring the distance between them by way of trigonometric triangulations. (If you know the exact distance between two points and the angles with a third point - then you can calculate the distance of the third point. Think Pythogoras theorem.)

Triangulation surveys were based on a few carefully measured baselines and a series of angles. The initial baseline was measured with great care since the accuracy of the subsequent survey was critically dependent upon it. Various corrections were applied, principally temperature. An especially accurate folding chain was used, laid on horizontal tables, all shaded from the sun and with constant tension - so  that they not expand or contract from the heat or loose their exact length by loosening of the links. The Great Trigonometrical Survey of India started on 10 April 1802 with the measurement of a baseline near Madras. Major Lambton selected the flat plains with St. Thomas Mount at the north end and Perumbauk hill at the southern end. The baseline was 7.5 miles (12.1 km) long.

After they had that baseline, one officer was despatched to find high vantage points on the hills of the west so that the coastal points of Tellicherry and Cannanore could be connected. The high hills chosen were Mount Delly and Tadiandamol. The distance from coast to coast was 360 miles (580 km) and this survey line was completed in 1806.

This was an insanely painstaking and difficult job, and luckily for them, Lambton turned out to be the perfect anal guy to do it. He trained a whole team of indians to be surveyors - these guys came to be known as 'pandits', or 'learned people' and they walked all across South India, lugging their giant instruments and pulling them up steep mountains or temple tops or church steeples and peering through them to measure distant points where another team of goat-footed pandits had climbed up and planted a flag. The locals thought that either they were completely out of their gourds, or were doing foul black magic of some sort, or were just going to a high point to be able to look over walls and letch at their women in the nuddy! Many times the surveyors had to run for their lives, being chased by tigers or bears or wild buffalo - or by enraged villagers. The sheer difficulty of the job is unimaginable today.

CALCUTTA BASE LINE

The project started in 1802, and they thought that it would be done in 5 years. It ended up taking 70 years! By that time, there had been the Great Sepoy Mutiny/

First war of Indian Independence in 1857 (pick one as per your point of view) and the East India company had been nationalised, and the British crown had taken over.

The government had been so pleased with the result of the south indian survey that the project was expanded to become a survey of all India. Lambton retired in due course of time after a long and glittering career, and was replaced by his deputy - George Everest.. He led the survey to map out these trigonometric 'gridiron lines' all across India - from Kashmir to Kanyakumari, from Sindh to Assam! A most amazing feat.

This was the first time that India had been accurately measured - and these measurements are used by the Indian government to this day. Among the many accomplishments of the Survey were the demarcation of the British territories in India and the measurement of the height of the Himalayan giants: Everest, K2, and Kanchenjunga. The Survey had an enormous scientific impact as well, being responsible for one of the first accurate measurements of a section of an arc of longitude, and for measurements of the geodesic anomaly - the effects of mountain masses on the earth's gravitational field -

which led to the development of the theories of isostasy (the state of gravitational equilibrium between the Earth's crush and mantle) - both of which are essential to modern mapping techniques and GPS navigation. It is so fascinating to think that measuring the ground with bits of chain finally led to Google maps and Uber!

I would recommend a book called 'The Great Arc' by the eminent historian John Keay, to know the story of how this happened. It was truly a monumental effort and is an amazing read.

Anyway - coming back to the Himalayas. About the same time as Lambton was starting on his survey of South India in 1805, 1200 miles to the North another surveyor called Charles Crawford had entered the kingdom of Nepal and was peering with professional curiosity at the massive mountains he saw there. Earlier people had thought that these snow covered peaks were not all that tall - but when the trained eye of surveyor Crawford fell on them, he realised that they are very far away - and must be very tall indeed!

He took readings and measurements and stuff which seemed to show peaks of extra-ordinary heights! 11000 to 20000 feet above stations of observation! These numbers electrified the western world - but unfortunately the journals and precise observations of Crawford were lost. But at least they knew that the Himalayas were not active volcanos as thought earlier - the white plumes seen above them were snow, and not steam.

But unfortunately for the curiosity of the west, the Anglo-Nepal friendship treaty was cancelled in 1804 - the Nepalese king saw the British conquest of India with horror and closed the border to prevent the same thing from happening to him - and the border was closed to westerners for the next 150 years - leaving the gasping scientist in the same position of a teenage boy rudely pulled away from peering through the window of an undressing girl. Frustrated and filled with longing for more information.

Various white people kept peering at the mountains from their haunts in the Gangetic plains and trying to take observations of the far-off mountains - and soon had enough data to confidently say that these Himalayan ranges were definitely the loftiest in the world and its peaks were much higher than those in the Andes. But since both Nepal and Tibet - the homes of these mountains - remained xenophobic and cut-off from the world, all these numbers were approximations at best.

But as British domination increased more and more in India, the surveyors could get closer and closer to the mountains and get more and more accurate numbers. George Everest was so obsessed with measuring the peaks that he relocated the headquarters of the Indian Survey to the hill-station of Mussoorie, in the foothills of the Himalayas. His headquarters were called 'Logarithm lodge' in a place called 'Hathipaon' - and he and his team of surveyors and mapmakers and calculators laboured away there. His teams of 'compass-walas' went tirelessly all over the hills, taking measurements and planting potatoes wherever they went. The potato - a south american root vegetable - had been identified by the then Governor-General of India as being an important contribution to Himalayan diet and economy. It is interesting to note that today almost everything about the Great Survey has been forgotten in India, Logarithm lodge lies in ruins and British rule is long gone - but the potato still rules supreme as an integral part of Himalayan diets.

Anyway - coming finally the point of Mt Everest - the British surveyors painstakingly measured the heights of hundreds of imposing Himalayan peaks and were flabbergasted to find not one, but many peaks above 8000 meters in height! For a time they thought that Nanda devi was the highest peak in the world, then they found that Kanchenjunga is even higher. But then they found another peak behind Kanchenjunga which seemed to be even higher!

They couldn't find a local name for it, so they gave it a working name of 'gamma'. It took them several years and a lot of frustrated attempts - but finally James Nicholson was able to get a clear reading of it. Numerous angles, both vertical and horizontal, were taken and finally 6 angles were used in the final calculations. All these calculations were done by human minds, as there were no calculators or computers around, of course - and the best human computers were the Indians.

Finally, the chief computer - an Indian arithmetic genius called Radhanath Sickdhar - came to the conclusion that they had found the world's highest peak!

The Surveyor-General at the time was Sir George Everest's successor - Andrew Scott Waugh - and he made the most unusual suggestion of naming the peak after his predecessor and mentor, Sir George Everest. This was a most unusual thing, because naming conventions of the day strongly favoured finding the local name of the mountain and using that - but Waugh said that there was no local name for it and so he could name it as he damn pleased.

'Not true' - some people said - 'It is called Chomolungma or Devadhanga by the poor sods who stay there' but it was too difficult to write such a long name on the maps, so the Everest name was there to stay and so it remains to this day.

The Nepali government tried to rename

it as 'Sagarmatha' - but no one knows or cares. Everest it is.

The man it was named after was long gone by then - gone home that is, not dead. He went back to England and rode in the local hunt and got married and presumably enjoyed the local…er….I forget what I was going to say…

He married at 55, to a girl half his age - and it is a tribute to his virility and fitness that he fathered 6 children after that! He was already a legendary figure in the world of scientific exploration, and he grew a great big bushy beard and hung out with the great science men of the day, like explorer David Livingstone and chemist Micheal Faraday - and no doubt simpered bashfully whenever people congratulated him on having the world's tallest mountain named after him. He died in London aged 76 and was buried in Hove, near Brighton.

No memorial was ever erected to him, and he and William Lambton and the Great Arc were soon forgotten. But because his successor had great respect for him and named a mountain after him - his name lives on and is known around the world - so what if it is a bit mispronounced?

He even has a masala brand named after him! Now that is fame which he would never have expected!

**Deorali to Trakshindo**

The next morning dawned - the sun came up and the cock was just drawing in a deep breath to start crowing, when a loud shout came from the room and made it lose it's train of thought.

'COCK A DOODLE.....SQUACK!!!'
'UTHO RE! UTHO RE! UTHO RE!'
'SQUACK!'

I jerked awake in shock, as did all the residents of Deorali village. The very snows of the Deorali pass rumbled in shock as the sound waves hit it.
'Whut…whit…what…' I gibbered in shock and opened my eyes to see Bharathi glaring at me.
'UTHO RE!' she bellowed, causing the cock to explode into a pile of feathers and the village dogs to run yelping away in fright. 'GET UP! THIS IS THE MOUNTAINS! YOU NEED TO GET AN EARLY START!'
'Wha…who…whu…' I said, sounding like a brain-damaged owl
'MOVE IT!'
'Yes ma'm.'

I jumped up and got out of bed and got ready in a trice. We left the hotel to see the village totally deserted. All the streets were empty - even the cows and pigs and yaks were missing. I looked around mystified, but Bharathi seemed to be used to it. She walked off with a jaunty stride and I staggered along with my gigantic backpack.

I thought I saw a foot sticking out of a hedge, and heard a whispered 'has she gone?', which was answered by a chorus of 'shhh shhh shhh' from various hiding places.

The route would continue to be an up and down route today - we had stayed near the pass, so the first part of the walk was all downhill, and so I enjoyed it tremendously. The alpine forests were really something, and the trail was in great condition. The weather was also great - blue skies, white clouds etc.

'What wonderful weather!' I said joyfully. I could have just skipped along like a lamb high on grass. (See what I did there? High five!)
'Yes - but don't depend on it.' Bharathi answered 'the weather in the mountains is notoriously fickle - it can change in an instant. And we have an hours worth of trail to make up because we did not reach our target yesterday.'
'Really?' I said, looking at the sky. 'The

weather seems great.'

'Bombay fashions and mountain seasons change in an instant' she said. I was so shocked at this scruffy hobbit talking about fashion that I almost tripped and fell on my face!

'Fashion? Really? You follow fashion?' I asked incredulously.

'I was just quoting a mountain saying.'
'Ah. Of course.'
'Why? Why can't I follow fashion?' she asked dangerously.

'No no no no…of course you can…I just….' I babbled nervously

'I know EVERYTHING!' she snarled at me. 'EVERYTHING! WHATEVER YOU SAY IS WRONG!'

'Yes yes yes…of course…'
'TELL ME THE NAME OF ALL THE 8000 METER PLUS PEAKS!'
'I…er….'
'TELL ME THE NAME OF THE FIRST PERSON TO SUMMIT A 8000ER.'
'I…er…'
'TELL ME THE TALLEST MOUNTAIN IN THE DHAULADAR RANGE'
'I…er…'
'BUHAHAHA! YOU KNOW NOTHING! NOTHING!'

I nodded smartly, like popo the puppet and this whole exchange cheered her up extremely and she walked on jauntily, whistling a few bars.

As we walked, she told me more of her adventures and I listened with wide-eyed admiration.

Her Thai visa was dying, so she had to do a 'renewal run' - which basically meant that she would exit the country, go for a stroll for a few minutes and then return back to the border and get it stamped again. She explored Mae Hong Son, the north-eastern border of Thailand, but was not too impressed by it as it was deemed 'too commercialised' , and anyway there was tension between Thailand and Myanmar, and they kept thinking that she is a Burmese illegal immigrant. So she abandoned the border and went deep inside to Chiang Mai - Thailand's second most important town. She explored a 'Jade factory' there, but was too cheap to actually buy any jade. They showed her some fantastic Sapphires and Rubies and Jade jewellery - but that was a classic example of 'pearls before swine'. All she could do there is to watch some free videos and then skedaddle. Then she went off to see the highest mountain in Thailand - Doi Inthanon - there were no buses or taxis to come back and she was standing in the rain and attempting to hitch-hike, when again the

Patron saint of idiots came to her aid and sent her a nice Kuwaiti family who not only gave her a lift, but also took her to see a couple of beautiful waterfalls.

    Soon it was time to leave Thailand - and Thailand heaved a huge sigh of relief, as she exited and entered Laos. Laos used to be a french possession - french Indo-china, and immediately all the signs were in French - Bienvenue a Lao PDR! Laos is dominated by the mighty Mekong river, and the place she was in - Huay Xai - was the apex of the golden triangle (intersection of Thailand, Laos and Burma). When she changed dollars for Lao Kip, she actually had to clear space in her backpack to store the cash - the exchange rate was 10,220 Lao kip to the dollar!

Now all transport was by boat on the river - as the Mekong had swallowed up the road in the monsoon, and would slowly regurgitate the digested and decayed road only after the waters receded post-monsoon. A 7 hour trip costed only 6 dollars. The foreigners complained about the dilapidated condition of the road - but hey - what can you expect in 6 dollars? A Star Virgo cruise?

    Laos is very undeveloped as compared to Thailand - but what it lost in creature comfort was made up by the charm of the relaxed pace of life and simplicity and unspoilt nature of the people. She enjoyed people watching, and as an Indian she was not as hassled by the basic state of things as the uptight firangs. The buses travelled only when full, and the seats were wooden planks and the passengers were a mix of people, rice sacks, hens, ducks and a whining dog. It would have included a squealing pig as well, but the driver objected. The bus was filled to capacity, and after that, the passengers clung to the outside of the bus like baby scorpions hitching a ride on mama scorpion. She had a great time reliving India travel as she made her way through Laos on bus and boat and when the locals learnt that she was from India, they would say 'Aaaaah… Buddha Buddha!' and bow to her as if she was personally responsible for the spread of Buddhism.

Laos is less touristy than Thailand, with all its positive and negative connotations. The landscape is pristine, Laos is 70% mountains and has a 74% forest cover. Since it was the rainy season, the scenery was MAGNIFICENT. The National Highway is Mekong and the state highways are also rivers. About the roads, the lesser said the better!

Laos is still the kind of place where hotel owners will still tie white threads to the wrists on departing guests and say a little prayer to wish them good luck.  On the flip side,   public transport was dismal on the muddy roads so much so that  people used the road only for places where the river wasn't going to.    Accommodation  was quite adequate  but meals were basic. It was more of eating enough to stay alive, and choosing between fried rice and noodles - and noodles and fried rice!

    Our trail wound all the way down to Kinja village, and I suddenly noticed all the trees were covered with giant spider webs. And on closer inspection, I realised that these webs have been made by truly gigantic spiders. Wow. All over the place there were these huge fracking spiders. Any person with arachnophobia would have fainted straightaway.

    I felt like Bilbo Baggins in the forest of Mirkwood, being attacked by the giant spiders. I was with a dwarf anyway… All I needed to do was become invisible by putting on my magic ring and start slashing them with my little elven sword.

    'Old fat spider spinning in a tree!
Old fat spider can't see me!
    Attercop! Attercop!
      Won't you stop,

Stop your spinning and look for me!'

I started singing, and Bharathi looked at me as if I had lost my mind.

'Er…sorry. LOTR reference…couldn't resist it. Have you read the 'The Lord of the Rings' by JRR Tolkein? It's my favourite book! There's this character called Bilbo Baggins and he…er….' I trailed off as she glared at me.

She hadn't read Tolkein, and immediately took it up as a challenge.

'HAVE YOU READ TOLSTOY?'
'I…er….no…'
'HAVE YOU READ DOSTOEVSKY?'
'I…er….no…'
'HAVE YOU READ SOLZHENITSYN?'
'I…er…no…'
'HA. YOU KNOW NOTHING! NOTHING!'
'I…er…'
'I WILL READ TOLKEIN AS SOON AS WE GET BACK, THEN I WILL KNOW MORE DILDO SONGS THAN YOU! HA!'
'Bilbo…'
'WHAT?'
'Er…Bilbo…not dildo…'
'YES. THAT!'

Those spiders - we referred to them as 'Kinja spiders' for a long time - were Giant Wood Spiders, which are found in tropical forests all over Asia. And also in Australia - because all the scary creatures of the world can be found in Australia. These can grow as big as a soup plate…and interestingly, it is only the female spiders which grow that big. The male spiders are so small that you can hardly see them! Makes you wonder about the mating…'Size does matter' and all that.

Even more interestingly, the males actually 'plug' the female's genitalia after sex with some sticky goo - so that no other spider can dip his wick for some time! Talk about a chastity belt. This plugging is also done by several other species - rodents, scorpions, mice, some monkeys - and even Kangaroos. Humans prefer marriage for the same result.

These spiders are so big that some tribes roast and eat them as a crunchy protein snack - which just proves that man can eat anything if he is hungry enough.

After Kinja, the trail started going uphill and it was a long hard walk to Sete village. I was trudging along, gasping and sweating - when it started to rain.

Bharathi immediately pulled out a raincoat. I just stood there.

'Where is your raincoat?' she asked. 'You came on a Himalayan trek without a raincoat?'

'I had no idea.' I replied. 'And anyway, it is not raining much. This is hardly a drizzle. In the Sahyadris we trek through pouring rain without any raincoats'

'You are not in the Sahyadris are you? This is the Himalayas and we are on a months trek, not a day trek. You have to guard your health.'

'Yes, but what to do? I don't have anything…come, let's carry on.' I said and started trudging.

'We will pick up something in the next settlement.' She said. There was no raincoat available - but she came back triumphantly holding a plastic packet.

'What will I do with a plastic packet?'

'It is like a sack… unfolds into a plastic sheet. You wear it over your head and wrap it around yourself and it keeps the rain out… see…all the locals are using it.'

And indeed they were…they either had a bamboo body cover lined with that plastic, or they were using just the plastic. I tried it, but it was so awkward to use …it kept sliding off or getting caught in something.

We finally made it to Sete village, and were enveloped in such which clouds and mists that we couldn't see five feet in front of us. It reminded me of the night at Harishchandragad.

'This is no good.' Bharathi said. 'We will have to stay in the first hotel we find.'

That first hotel turned out be a dump, unfortunately. The toilet was terrible and I refused to grace it with my bare ass.

But it was shelter, and food and a nice warm bed was available. We had a very late lunch and sat there chilling out till bed time. There was literally nothing to see - just a wall of white…so we slept off at 6 in the evening.

Because of this, we woke up at some unearthly hour - only to again see that unbroken wall of white! We dilly-dallied till about 8.30 AM and then decided to at least check out of that horrible lodge and go another cleaner place for breakfast.

While we had a rather over-priced breakfast, the weather cleared magically and we happily set out on the trail.

The first objective was Lamjura pass, which was at a fairly respectable hight of 3530 meters and we huffed and puffed to cross it. Or at least I did. Mountain passes are always cold due to the winds whooshing through the narrow gaps in the mountains and this was even colder due to the rains. What with the altitude and cold and the wind

and the rain, I developed chest congestion and wheezed and gasped as we negotiated the long and rocky descent from the pass.
GASP. WHEEZE. WHEEZE.

But it was downhill all the way to Junbesi village, and the sun came out and the clouds went away and we had brilliant views. It was a wonderful walk down, and Junbesi village was as pretty as a picture! Wow. Bucolic splendour!

We got rooms in a lovely lodge, and Bharathi was shocked when she heard the price.
'HOW MUCH?'
'20 rupees. Hee hee hee' the hostess twittered
'Twenty rupees? That's it?'
'Yes yes…only twenty Nepali rupees!'
We were gobsmacked. How could it be so cheap? We kept looking for the catch - but there was none. The room was clean and beautiful, the bedding was clean and the toilet was squeaky clean. There was a beautiful garden, with awesome views of Mt Numbur, and there was a heated lounge where we could relax and mingle with other guests, or just relax.

It was a wonderful deal and the only implied request was that we should eat in that lodge itself and not go anywhere else. The lodge would make its money on the food billing. We were happy to oblige - the food rates were the same everywhere, so there was no scam there either.

Everything was fine except for my chest congestion. I was not used to the altitude or the effort of trekking, and the getting wet with rain or sweat also must have aggravated it - so I wheezed all night. A nice day - but a bad night.

The warmth of the next day cleared up my chest, and the fresh air and the lovely views totally restored my spirits! What views! Man - that was amazing. The sheer scale of the mountains is amazing. And they are still friendly green mountains, so they don't overawe or scare you. The amazing mountain air and mountain views are like a tonic.

And by gum, you need that tonic - because the walking can be tough!

The first part of the day was very easy and enjoyable - as we descended all the way down to the Junbesi river and crossed it on a beautiful suspension bridge. The trail was full of these amazing suspension bridges which helped the travellers to cross the fast-flowing rivers without any problems.

The amazing thing about these bridges is that a lot of them are not made by the government but by the generous donations from the Gurkhas in the British army. They paid for the construction of these bridges as a charitable effort. It is an amazing experience to walk on these hanging bridges and stop in the middle and watch that river roaring merrily below. We were in the Tibetan buddhist areas now, and so the bridges were gaily festooned with colourful prayer flags.

The prayer flags are printed with the words of the Buddhist prayer 'Om Mani Padme Hum' and the locals believe that the wind blows these prayers all over the country when they make the flags flap. I thought that it was a perfectly wonderful concept.

That part of the walk was wonderful as we crossed the river and the ridge basking in the warm sunshine. But after that I developed a kink in my knee and started limping painfully. I bought a stick from some kids and used that to take the weight off my knee - but what with the chest wheezing and the knee paining I felt that I was fucked in both areas trekking - Lower body strength and Cardiovascular fitness!

And of course, it was just then that we had to cross another steep pass. We huffed up a steep slope and limped down a steep descent and of course the weather packed up as well.

We dropped our original plans and decided to stay in the first hotel we found in Trakshindo village. I limped and wheezed my way there and I crashed into the bed.

'Leave me MacDuff.' I gasped and wheezed. 'I am dying! Bury my heart at wounded knee! Tell my parents I loved them! Kiss me Hardy!'

'Oh nonsense.' Bharathi said, waving my groans aside. 'You are doing very well for a first time trekker. Some Tiger balm and a good nights rest will put you right.'

And it did! I felt much better after changing out of my sweaty clothes and smearing my knee and chest with the fiery Tiger balm, and we went off to visit the Trakshindo monastery in the evening.

The views were....you know it dude... amazing!

While I gasped and decompressed in

bed, my mind went back to the story of Everest and the long and fascinating history of climbing it - which led finally to the formation of this Everest base camp trek.

The intrepid British surveyors had discovered and announced Mount Everest to be the tallest peak in the world in 1850 - but soon they had more urgent things on their mind. In a short time, the whole of India was ablaze with the Great Sepoy Mutiny ( or the First War of Independence, as we call it nowadays) and the East India company had other things to think about than climbing mountains. The vicious attacks on the British and the far more vicious and sadistic reprisals on the natives by the British left the country in tatters - but after all the dust had died down, there was no doubt who was top dog. The British government threw away the fig leaf of the East India Company and assumed charge of India as a proper conquered domain and part of the British empire. Now the whole country was subservient to the British crown - either being directly ruled by it, or being wholly influenced by it.

One would have thought that the new Pax Brittanica would make it much easier for mountaineering expeditions to go and clamber up all sorts of mountains - but no.

Quite the opposite actually. Both Nepal and Tibet were quite horrified and scared shitless by what had happened to India, and firmly closed their borders to all foreigners - especially Britishers. Keep out. Fuck off.

The British government was initially quite happy to let the status quo be, because they had their hands full with managing the brand new Indian possessions and looting them as much as possible and stealing everything that was not actually nailed down. 'Loot' was the first Indian word to enter the Oxford english dictionary, so you can easily realise what was on the minds of the fine British gentlemen in the colonies. Bloody thieves, the lot of them.

But then internationally things were happening - and indeed had been building up for years and years. The Russian Tsars saw England getting fat on Indian gold, and thought that they should also get a piece of the colonial action. They pushed the boundaries of the Russian empire further and further into central Asia and swallowed up a number of the ancient Khanates - the ancient remnants of the Mongol empire ( which are now the 'Stans' - Kazakhstan, Uzbekistan etc) and indeed the whole of Siberia and ruled Asia from coast to coast!

The British were scared shitless! They were convinced that the cossacks were going to ride roughshod over the mountains and kick their butts and drink vodka out of their skulls unless they did something quick. So they decided to set up a ring of buffer states around their territories - they needed Afghanistan as a buffer from the west and Tibet as a buffer from north and east.

The problem was that neither Afghanistan nor Tibet wanted anything to do with any foreigners and threatened to cut off the heads of any damn firang who dared to put foot inside their countries. It was no idle threat, and the British didn't want to really piss them off.

But they wanted information and maps of Tibet. The whole of Tibet was an empty white patch on their maps, and they desperately wanted data. So what to do?

They came out with a very James Bond idea! They decided to train Indian pandits (the guys trained in map making by the Indian survey, which I mentioned earlier) as spies! Mission Impossible stuff.

This was the brainchild of Captain Thomas George Montgomerie, a young

Royal Engineers officer attached to the Survey of India. When he was posted in Ladakh, he noticed that natives of India passed freely backwards and forwards between Ladakh and Yarkand in Chinese Turkestan. Thus, why not send native explorers, handpicked for their intelligence and resourcefulness and trained in clandestine surveying techniques?

The sub-text also was that these natives were entirely expendable, and even if they were caught and executed it was not a big issue. The empire would be obliged to go to war if a British guy was caught and chopped up, but no one would greatly care if a native got the short end of the stick.

The first guinea pig for this was a muslim dude who was sent to Yarkand (now in China - then an independent kingdom) to do some surreptitious mapmaking. He died on the way - but he managed to make some very interesting maps and send them back to Montgomerie. WooHoo! Success!

Now the problem was how to get Indians into Tibet - the Indians were Hindus, and only Buddhists were allowed into Tibet. So they established a spy school and they trained the pandits to pretend to be Buddhist monks and join various caravans to enter tibet - they could pretend to be visiting monasteries or be doing a pilgrimage to Lhasa or whatever was convenient.

They were trained to walk at a constant pace - so that they covered a precise distance per step. Then all they had to do was to count the number of steps and they would know the exact distance they had covered, and keep track of the numbers by using the prayer beads. They were given high tech spy equipment of the day - spy-type prayer wheels - with compasses hidden on top, and places to write and hide notations, and mini-telescopes, thermometers and all kinds of cool stuff.

These spy-cum-surveyors actually managed to penetrate into Tibet…into Lhasa itself - collect all sorts of interesting information, create maps, measure altitudes and managed to come back alive! It was a most thrilling and audacious venture - it was utter madness, and amazingly - it managed to deliver!

These stories are amazingly well told in the book 'Trespassers on the roof of the world - the race for Lhasa' by Peter Hopkirk. It's an amazing book, and it is available on Kindle.

To quote a few words from the book - 'As the heavily laden caravan wound it's way from through the snow-filled valleys and passes of Southern Tibet towards Lhasa, a solitary Buddhist pilgrim, rosary in hand, could be observed toiling alongside the straining yaks. As he strode his companions could hear him repeating the endlessly the sacred Tibetan mantra 'Om Mani Padme Hum'. Sometimes he would draw a prayer wheel from the folds of his thick sheepskin coat and rotate it with a flick of his wrist for hour after hour, filling the thin Tibetan air with prayer. Conscious of their pious companion's need for privacy, the Ladakhi craven men avoided questioning or talking to him at such times.

What they did not know, and never did discover, was that this was no Buddhist holy man. Had they suspected this and troubled to count the beads of his rosary, they would have found that there were only a hundred of these, rather than the sacred one hundred and eight. Had they removed the top from his prayer wheel while he slept, they would have discovered, instead of the usual scroll bearing block-printed prayers, tiny pencilled figures and mysterious jottings in Urdu.

Once their suspicions had been aroused, they might have noticed that sometimes this holy man dropped behind the slow-moving caravan. Then he would remove surreptitiously from his sleeve, a small, curious looking device made of metal and glass, through which he would peer hastily at some distant feature, afterwards scribbling a brief note which he would then conceal inside his prayer wheel. At other time, after making sure he was not being observed, he would remove from the top of his pilgrims staff a thin glass object (which some of his companions might have recognised as a thermometer) and dip it fleetingly into a boiling kettle or cooking vessel. Again, he would note down the reading an hurriedly secrete this in his prayer-wheel.

Not merely was this traveller not a Buddhist, but neither was he a holy man. He was a HIndu - and worse, he was a British spy. Had his identity been discovered, he would undoubtedly have been killed on the spot.'

Isn't that great stuff, or what?

One of these pundits was a guy called Nain Singh Rawat - he surveyed the trade route from Nepal to Tibet, determined for the first time the location and altitude of Lhasa and surveyed a large section of the Brahmaputra. He walked 1580 miles -

31600000 paces exactly! He was a legendary 'spy explorer' and has a mountain range in Ladakh named after him. The Indian government even issued a postage stamp honouring him in 2004. His brothers were also in the game - Mani singh and Krishna Singh - and they were all honoured by the Royal Geographic Society of London.

There was another Bengali gentleman called Sarat Chandra Das, who not only managed to enter Tibet - but managed to settle down and live in Lhasa. Unlike the pandits, who were simple villagers, Sarat

Chandra was an educated man - he was an alumnus of Presidency college, Calcutta and was headmaster of the Bhutia boarding school in Darjeeling. In 1878, he made friends with a Tibetan lama called Ugyen Gyatso, and managed to get a passport to go to Tibet and study in the monastery of Tashilhunpo. He remained in Tibet for six months, studying Tibetan and Sanskrit texts and became a respected scholar. He returned to Tibet one more time with Lama Ugyen, where he explored the Yarlung valley and even prepared the first ever Tibetan-English dictionary.

But what the innocent Lama Ugyen did not know, was that Sarat babu was actually a spy for the British, accompanying Colman Macaulay on his 1884 expedition to Tibet to gather information on the Tibetans, Russians and Chinese. After he left Tibet, the reasons for his visit were discovered and many of the Tibetans who had befriended him suffered severe reprisals. And as we noted earlier - the reprisals in Tibet were very severe indeed.

To quote the author Laurence Austin Waddell - 'The ruin thus brought about by the Babu's visit extended also to the unfortunate Lama's relatives, the governor of Gyantsé (the Phal Dahpön) and his wife

(Lha-cham), whom he had persuaded to befriend Sarat C. Das. These two were cast into prison for life, and their estates confiscated, and several of their servants were barbarously mutilated, their hands and feet were cut off and their eyes gouged out, and they were then left to die a lingering death in agony, so bitterly cruel was the resentment of the Lamas against all who assisted the Babu in this attempt to spy into their sacred city.'

Sarat himself was much feted and respected by the British, and lived happily in Darjeeling in a house which he called 'The Lhasa villa' and hosted a number of eminent visitors who were curious about his adventures.

These amazing stories should be common knowledge - but alas, they are almost completely forgotten in India today.

But the characters inspired by them live on in Rudyard Kipling's epic novel 'Kim' - which is a story of a kid who gets involved in the 'Great Game' - and gets trained in surveying and spy work by various people working in clandestine establishments. The character of 'Hurree Chunder Mookerjee' - a dude who looks like a servile fat Bengali at first glance, but is actually a super spy and surveyor in reality - is based on these brave pandits.

I just re-read 'Kim' today, and I was blown away by how great the book is. Kipling today is sometimes derided as being racist and 'empirist' (is that a word?) - but that is unfair. You should not judge ancient writers by modern standards. In fact, I was touched by the affection, empathy and admiration he had for India and Indians.

Anyway - coming back to Tibet - why is this long story relevant to the story of Everest base camp?

For the simple reason that since Nepal was closed tight - the only way to reach Everest was via Tibet. The mountain is on the border between Nepal and Tibet (the border actually runs through the top of Mt Everest) and you can access it from both countries.

Tibet was also closed equally tight - but now the times were changing. These pandits were only the first people to enter and map Tibet - but they would not be the last. The allure of the hidden kingdom on the 'Roof of the world' gave all kinds of people a hard-on for the place - political agents, explorers, adventurers, mountaineers and evangelical

Christians.

One guy even planned to fly into Tibet, crash land his plane on Everest and run up to the summit and plant Britain's flag on top - but luckily for him, the government got wind of his plans and grounded his plane at the airport.

Tibet rebuffed all of them - some gently, some not so gently, and some were chopped up and thrown into the river.

But the guy who finally ripped Tibet open and forced it to talk to the British empire was one of the supermen of that heroic British age - Sir Francis Younghusband! He was a true superman of that age, and had earned great fame by the age of 25 as he carried out several daring and adventurous journeys in Central Asia - in China, Mongolia and the 'stans - and even crossed the Taklamakan and Gobi deserts. He was also an accomplished player of the 'Great Game', having completed several secret missions in sensitive areas.

Thus he was the perfect person for the then Viceroy of India, Lord Curzon, to send to Tibet to demand them to have diplomatic relations with Britain. Curzon had become totally paranoid about Russian influence in

Tibet and was terribly concerned that Tibet was going to ally itself with Russia - and he ordered Younghusband to enter Tibet - by force, if necessary - and force them to talk to Britain.

It was absolutely impossible - as Tibet was ringed with massive natural defences of impassable mountains, had a fanatically loyal citizenry, a large(ish) army - and the whole landscape was a desert - with no food for man or grass for beasts.

But Younghusband did the impossible - he got his army - and his big guns - over the mountains, all the way to Lhasa - the forbidden city - demonstrated the fearful power of his modern guns and armaments and forced the Tibetans to come to terms with him in 1903 -04.

And he did another impossible thing - he managed to convince the Tibetans that he was not an enemy and that the British were not bad people. His army had indeed gunned down hundreds of Tibetans - but only after warning them several times. And after that battle, his doctors treated all the tibetan wounded and sick and saved the lives of many. Younghusband did not rape Lhasa, he did not allow any looting and he treated the Dalai Lama and his court with a lot of respect.

This made the Dalai Lama look at the British differently, and this was a good thing for him - as they saved his life and his throne the very next year! The Chinese empire heard of the British excursion to Tibet, and became hopping mad, as they believed that Tibet was part of the Chinese empire and they had no business talking to Britain directly! So they decided to invade Tibet and rough up the Dalai Lama to remind him who was boss.

The very next year they invaded Tibet - in 1905- and the then Dalai Lama was forced to flee into British territories for safety. Oh, the irony. He had to flee to the same guys who had invaded him, because now another guy was invading him.

The Dalai Lama was treated with a lot of respect and consideration by the British resident for several years - till he was able to return to Tibet in 1911. This convinced the Dalai Lama that the British were OK people, and so he allowed British expeditions to make an attempt to find and climb the fabled Mount Everest.

The road to Everest was finally open - but from the Tibet side.

**Trakshindo to Phakding**

I slept well that night - no doubt due to merit accumulated by the visit to Trakshindo monastery the earlier evening. I had a headache every time I woke, but managed to drop off again into a refreshing sleep.

'The Buddha has blessed me!' I cried to Bharathi. 'Let us light more butter lamps in the monastery.'
'Oh balls.' She replied. 'You are just acclimatising, that's all. The Buddha had nothing to do with it. Keep shut and start walking.'
'Yes Ma'm.'

It was a wonderful experience very day to shoulder the backpack and get on the trail. It was just so beautiful - it took my breath away every time. Was I really doing this? Was I really trekking in the Nepal Himalayas? Was I really seeing such beauty? Was I really enjoying this fearsome girl's company so much? Or was I dreaming, and would soon wake up and have to get back to my daily office drudgery? Let me enjoy this dream as much as I can before I wake up. I would take a deep breath of that incomparable mountain air, and look around those amazing green mountains.

We had woken up early, as is normal in the mountains and had enjoyed the divine sunrise - the sun coming up over the snow capped peaks ... Bharathi would point them out and name them to me - Numbur, Kangka etc. I wouldn't know one snowcap from another, but for her each peak was like an old friend - with its own identity, personality and quirks.

I was just lost in the beauty of it all, when the hotel owner handed me a cup of tea. Ah! The finishing touch! A refreshing cup of chai to aid the mind in appreciating this. I took a sip…

AAGHH
PTHOOO

This was the most disgusting brew in the whole world. This was not tea - it was pitiless torture of tea leaves and powdered milk. UGH. My tongue tried to choke me for making it taste such stuff. I was gasping… GAK GAK …

'How is the tea sir?' the owner asked me proudly - and she was such a sweet person that I couldn't bear to tell her that even dishwater would be a great improvement. I gave her a ghastly smile and assured her that it was great - perfect - and hastily chucked into the bushes when she wasn't looking.

'Come come…' I whispered to Bharathi. 'Let's move it before she makes another cup.'

It was a wonderful day - the winter of our discontent had been made glorious by the sun of York, so to speak, and we had a great time walking to the next village. A lot of my clothes had become soaked with sweat over past few days as I had perspired rather freely while clambering up and down the mountains - and had not really had a chance to dry - so I decided to take advantage of the right sunshine and tied them all over my backpack - and this must have presented a very curious sight to the locals.

A bald ruffian with a giant blue backpack with stinky clothes hung all over it, with a small black attack dog for company. Oh wait - that's not an attack dog! It's much worse….its…its…BHARATHI….AAAGH… RUN - RUN FOR YOUR LIVES!

We had a long descent down to Nuntala village, and continued to descent until we reached the Dudh Kosi river. What a beautiful sight! I was entranced! Even Bharathi - who had seen many beautiful places of the world -  was entranced!

The Kosi is one of the most important rivers of Nepal, and is formed by 7 tributaries - one of which was this one, the Dudh Kosi - 'the milky white river'. It was so named because it was literally white water, as the powerful current foamed all over the rocky mountain beds. These waters come directly from  the snowmelt of Mount Everest itself - and so have a special appeal to adventurers. Intrepid people have been doing white-water rafting and kayaking here since 1973! It has been described as having 'Grand Canyon-size walls with giant Himalayan peaks stacked on top' and is something really amazing.

We crossed the river on yet another of those amazing suspension bridges - you have so many of them in Nepal - and stopped for some time to take in the views. Ah! What a sight! What a feeling! That river is super-powerful, especially in the spring when the snows melt - and has brought down gigantic cathedral-sized rocks and boulders and flows over them with gay abandon. Before the days of suspension bridges, it must been an impossible task to ford these rivers…go all the way down, almost drown or die of hypothermia or get swept away as you cross that river and then huff and puff all the way up!

Then it was time to pay the price of that wonderful downhill walk and sights of the scenic river - a long long uphill walk to the next village. The Jiri - Lukla trail was basically an up and down trail - you cross a number of river and mountains - you walk up that mountain and then down to the river, and then again up another mountain and down another river - but don't gain much altitude. But it is very beautiful, and very empty. Most trekkers fly down to Lukla and start trekking from there, so this part of the trail was fairly empty and a joy to walk on.

Another reason for the trails to be empty was the threat of the Maoist revolutionary movement. Though mostly invisible to us, the communist guerilllas had been fighting a war with the government for decades, and they were a real power in these hilly areas. The Nepali Communist party had been waging a violent civil war against the government (no doubt funded and armed by Communist China) which had caused thousands of deaths so far. The Maoists controlled the hills and the Army controlled the plains and neither could break through.

The political situation in Nepal was in a very delicate situation, due to the terrible massacre of the royal family of Nepal. The king of Nepal at that time had been a well-loved figure - King Birendra. Well, the Maoists didn't love him - but the rest of the country did. His son - Dipendra - wanted to marry a non-Nepali girl whom he had met in the UK, and his parents were not on board with it. The girl was from an Indian royal family, and were apparently much richer than the Nepali Ranas - and the king didn't like that much. He was afraid that the girl would dominate the kid, and when he became King - India would dominate Nepal! So he firmly nixed the idea, and left the prince sick as mud.

What happened next was like a scene from a dystopian movie! Dipendra got coked up and high on something very dangerous - and picked up a machine gun, marched into the royal palace  - and shot his entire family dead!

12 members of the royal family were murdered in an instant, including his father - the king - and his mother - the queen - and his younger brother and sister! After that, Dipendra turned the gun on himself and committed suicide!

This shocked the whole country and rocked the nation to its core.

The only member of the royal family left alive was an uncle nobody liked and hence was not invited to that royal dinner - Gyanendra, and he was a most unpopular figure in Nepal. But he was the only choice left and so he was crowned king.

There were many rumours after this that there was a terrible plot involved and Dipendra was not the killer and there was more to the story than was released to the press - but the damage was done. The King - and his entire family - were dead.

The maoists took full advantage of this terrible tragedy and the fact of the  new king Gyanendra  being a most unpopular figure in Nepal and stepped up their war - and so Nepal was reeling under tragedy after tragedy.

The tourists and trekkers obviously did not want to get caught in the crossfire, so most of them avoided this part of the EBC and flew in directly to Lukla. But I must say that apart from seeing a sign painted on a wall - which I could not read as it was in Nepali…but it had the hammer and sickle thingy - we saw no signs of anything amiss, and the locals were so smiling and friendly that it was difficult as thinking of people like these being leftist killers.

Because there were comparatively few trekkers on the trail, we kept seeing the same faces and we smiled and nodded, and occasionally chatted. There was an American guy who kept telling the locals that he was from Canada, in order not to attract unwelcome attention from any Communists. There was a French group - they were much older than us, and smokers to boot - but they always ended up finishing the hike faster than us. There was an extraordinarily handsome American who looked like Brad Pitt who must have a trail of broken hearts all over the mountains. There were a lot of Scandinavians and Europeans who kept to themselves as they didn't speak much english.

We found a little chess set in the hotel and decided to play in the evening - and I discovered that she was crazily competitive! Maniacally so!

I beat her a couple of times and she refused to let me go after that until she had a chance to beat me!

'But…but…it's time for dinner.' I said, edging away from the table

'JUST SIT YOUR ASS DOWN' she growled at me, looking like a deranged werewolf

'But the kitchen will close…' I whined 'Dinner…'

'JUST ARRANGE THE PIECES YOU WORM! YOU …YOU…CHEATER…'

'But we have to have an early start…'

'HOW DARE YOU BEAT ME? I AM THE BEST! I KNOW EVERYTHING! I TAUGHT KARPOV AND KASPAROV! I ATE VISHWANATHAN ANAND FOR DINNER! NO ONE CAN BEAT ME! AAARGGHHH!'

She wouldn't let me go until she won a game, and I was worried that she would go totally bonkers and start taking bites out of my leg if she lost any more games. When finally she won a game (I let her win…but don't tell her that, OK? It's our little secret…) she let out a triumphant howl and scared everyone in the lounge!

'BUHAHAHAH! I WON! YOU LOST! I WON! I AM THE GREATEST! I AM THE CHAMPION!'

Good grief! I would have to lose to her everyday now, if I wanted any sleep at all.

To distract her, I asked her to continue her tales from the road - we had stopped last time in Laos.

The next day she made her way to Luang Prabang, in one of those local buses full of people and livestock and cargo, and will not leave until it is packed to the gills. (I always wondered about that expression… why packed to the 'gills' ? It's not as if fish are used as beasts of burden. Strange…)
Finally they made it to Luang Prabang - a UNESCO world heritage site - nestling on the confluence of 1.5km wide Mekong and 0.5km wide Nam Khan rivers, with hills all around, loads of beautiful temples and French colonial architecture. She loved the place and stayed there for 4 days, soaking up the atmosphere and the good food - it was an oasis of good food after 10 days in north Laos. She climbed the local mountain (of course) and explored the local Pak Ou caves, which are full of Buddhas in various shapes, sizes, postures and levels of deterioration. She attended a local dance program at the Royal theatre, where tiny female dancers lifted giant buckets of water with their teeth and continued dancing gracefully for 10 minutes! After the show

they invited the tourists to try it, and even hulking body builders couldn't do it. Our little iron-jaws was among the few who could lift the bucket - but only for 10 seconds.

While walking on the road, she was hailed by someone and when she turned around wondering who could know here in Luang Prabang, it turned out to be the Tamilian proprietor of the only Indian restaurant in the place. They were very happy to see a fellow Indian - and a Tamilian to boot - and treated her to an indian-style filter coffee. Later she went and saw the royal palace - a lovely grand structure - and was struck by the fact that the King and Queen were captured by the Communists and starved to death. Talk about vicissitudes of life!

Then she started out for Vientaine, and decided to stay in a town called Vang Vieng en route. It turned out that VV was a kayaking hotspot, and so she signed up for a full day of canoeing, caving and jumping into the river. There she casually mentioned that she had kayaked in the Indian ocean - and everyone went wow! You have kayaked in the Indian ocean! - And insisted that she take a solo canoe.

Unfortunately she was better at yakking than kayaking, and was unable to make the little boat go forward - paddle as hard as she may! But she got the hang of it after a good deal of swearing and sweating, and by the end of the day she was paddling like a pro! She jumped from a 25 feet high platform into the fast flowing river and swam into deep caves and faced and conquered all her fears - water, enclosed places, humiliation - and conquered them, and had a great day.

She found another Tamilian origin hotelier in the evening who was very glad to see her and yak away in Tamil and she was touched when he gave 4 free bananas along with her pancake.

The next day she made her way to Vientaine, and enjoyed several days of chilling on the river-front. She met an American lady she had helped out earlier, and was invited to stay at her house for as long as she was in town. She had to wait 4 days for her Cambodian visa to be issued, so she had four days of wat-hopping, riverfront chilling and hogging - and provided a place for her to relax for a bit after a frenetic travel routine.

Then it was on to Cambodia! She enjoyed travelling on the Mekong and seeing some spectacular Khmer temple ruins and lovely island hopping on that giant

14 km wide river until she landed up at the Cambodian border.

It was bedtime now, and we agreed to continue the story later.

The next day we were to go from Kharikhola to Surkhe, and I woke up full of beans after an excellent night - no wheezing, no problems - a most soothing 9 hours of knitting up the ravelled sleeve of care. (Or is unravelled sleeve? I forget)
But when I got all set to leave, I was at a stand! Where was Bharathi? She was gone! Gone! Gone! I was left alone! I didn't know whether to burst into tears at being abandoned, or dance a jig.

Well, I didn't want to scar the locals by seeing me dance a jig, so I started walking and just as I was enjoying that blessed feeling of freedom…FREEDOM!…I saw her waiting at the Kharikhola bridge and glaring at me.

I wanted to upbraid her for abandoning me, but she beat me to the draw.
'WHERE WERE YOU?' she growled.
'I…er….'
'YOU THINK YOU CAN ESCAPE ME? BUHAHAHAHA…NO ONE CAN ESCAPE ME! COME, YOU DOG! START WALKING!'

It was another wonderful day, and we enjoyed wonderful views as we climbed up a long slope to Bupa, and then skated down a long descent through a beautiful forest. The trees were covered with 'Old Mans beard' - a lichen or moss of some kind that grew all over the trees and made them look like elderly Ents from 'Lord of the Rings'.

I could just imagine them marching out of Fangorn forest to assault Saruman's lair in Isengard.

'We come, we come with roll of drum: ta-runda runda runda rom!
We come, we come with horn and drum: ta-rūna rūna rūna rom!
To Isengard! Though Isengard be ringed and barred with doors of stone;
Though Isengard be strong and hard, as cold as stone and bare as bone,
We go, we go, we go to war, to hew the stone and break the door;
For bole and bough are burning now, the furnace roars - we go to war!
To land of gloom with tramp of doom, with roll of drum, we come, we come;
To Isengard with doom we come!
With doom we come, with doom we come!'

I tried to explain it to Bharathi, but drew a blank.

'They look like Ents' I said

'Ain't what?'

'Ent …not…ain't' I tried to explain, but all I got was a glare.

'MARCH, YOU FOOL!'

And so we marched through that Entwood - like the Ent and the Entwife.

'When Spring unfolds the beechen leaf, and sap is in the bough;

When light is on the wild-wood stream, and wind is on the brow;

When stride is long, and breath is deep, and keen the mountain-air,

Come back to me! Come back to me, and say my land is fair!'

'Together we will take the road that leads into the West,

And far away will find a land where both our hearts may rest.'

We walked a long way that day - far more than normal. We normally used to wind up by lunch time, but we didn't like the look of the place we reached at noon and I was feeling quite fit and strong so we went on marching till the evening and stayed at a 'Luxurious' lodge (that's what they said in their sign boards) the Yak and Yeti at Surkhe. The lodge was very nice - it had lovely views and a western loo.

I was getting sick of the food though - it was mostly the traditional 'daal baat' - rice and lentils and potato, or some tasteless imitation of western food. The menu's used to be very inviting - sometimes multiple pages…but it turned out to be more of a fantasy of what the cook hoped to make some day, rather than what he could actually make. Hill food was entirely too bland for my spice-fed palate and I used to stare sadly at the food everyday.

Bharathi stared at me in amazement when I complained about the food.
'Are you mad? You are getting hot fresh food - which you did not have to carry and cook - and you are complaining? When we trek in India, we have to carry our own supplies, our own pots and pans, our own pressure cooker and firewood and our own eating utensils! At the end of a tiring day you have to make camp, chop and clean, make the food, wash the utensils, pack and unpack…here you are getting everything served to you on a platter and you are complaining? Spoilt brat!'

I sighed. It was all true - but the tongue

wants what the tongue wants.

The next day was the last day of the Jiri - Lukla section. We would be walking from Surkhe to Phakding and joining the main route. The crowds (well...comparatively) would increase and we would lose this splendid isolation and beautiful empty trails.

I couldn't even begin to tell you how much I had enjoyed this trip. It was something I had never done before, and the risk of jumping into unknown waters with an unknown person had totally paid off. I loved walking with this crazy little titch and loved the beauty of the mountains.

The middle altitude Himalayas were really beautiful and the villages were like something out of Hobbiton. Green fields, lovely traditional houses, friendly laughing people, streams and rivers - Bharathi pooh-poohed me when I talked about buying bottled water.

'Are you crazy? Just drink from the streams! This is original Himalayan water. Back home people pay big money to drink bottles of this water.'

Well - that was true. We even have a brand of water called 'Himalayan'. I just filled my bottle from a stream and drank it and it was absolutely wonderful! It was refreshingly cold, with a taste of the rocks of the mountains. This was water with personality - not the bland processed stuff we drink in the cities. It was a pleasure and a privilege to drink this water. I never even mentioned bottled or purified water again.

Every now and then we would find villagers selling tea or soft drinks, and the singsong voice of the seller was a pleasure to hear.
'Hot Lemon, cold lemon…hot grape, cold grape…tea, coffee…'
We would stop frequently and sip hot lemon or grape and soak in the views and enjoy each others company. Bharathi would tell me about her adventures and I would listen open-mouthed at her stories.

She had cycled from Bombay to Pune on an ancient hired single-speed bicycle. She had trekked and backpacked all across India to all kinds of obscure places. She was an engineer and an MBA - and while doing her MBA, she had seen a Bollywood movie set in Kashmir - 'Roja'. The locales fascinated her and so she immediately decided to cut classes and go to Kashmir.

'Are you crazy?' her classmates were shocked 'The blaze is ablaze with terrorism!' And indeed those were the heydays of terrorist activity in Kashmir and it was extremely dangerous.

'That's great!' Bharathi had responded.

'That means that there will be no tourists, and accommodation will be cheap!'

She landed in Srinagar and the hotel owner gave her his best room - the whole hotel was empty anyway.

'Sleep on this side of the bed - not that one.'

'Why?'

'In case of bullets, of course. Occasionally a stray bullet comes through that window.'

We had a very relaxed walk and reached Phakding by lunch time. This was the last day of low crowds, so we decided to enjoy it as much as possible and stay outside the main village to have the hotel to ourselves. We were the only people in the hotel when we checked in and were feeling proud of ourselves - but then it seemed that everyone had the same idea and a whole flood of firangs checked in as well.

The great appeal of the hotel was that they had a hot shower - and after a week on the road without a bath, that sounded very appealing indeed! Since we were the first check-ins, I had dibs on the shower and went in and had a long hot shower and even washed some clothes. What I didn't realise was that this was not an electric geyser with unlimited heating - it was a wood-fired heater, and I had finished off all the hot water. All the others who came haring up with towels and anticipation let out anguished yells as they were drenched with icy-cold water instead of the anticipated hot water and there was a lot of cursing.

Luckily no one identified me as the culprit, else I would have been beaten up for sure.

But it was all good in the end - the water warmed up in its own time and everyone had their shower - albeit a bit later than they thought. Everyone was mellow and happy and we had a relaxed evening sitting around in the lounge.

Our up-and-down walk was over, and soon we would be hitting the core of the Everest Base Camp trek and seeing some awesome altitudes.

The first Everest expeditions were not from the Nepal side, as it was still sewn up 'tight as a gnats asshole' as a colourful proverb puts it - but from Tibet, where a grateful Dalai Lama had graciously allowed British mountaineers to explore the Everest region. He gave them a special passport bearing the Great Red Seal of the Holy rulers of Tibet, which read 'Be it known to officers and headman…a party of sahibs will come to the sacred mountain…you shall render all help and safeguard them…the Dalai Lama is now on great friendly terms with the Government of India…'

At that time, before you could climb a mountain - you had to find it. And Everest was not easy to find, let alone climb. It is right at the border of Tibet, in the midst of a full court of very tall mountains.

In 1921 a small reconnaissance party entered into Tibet from Sikkim, one of the members of which would become one of the best known mountaineers in the world - a certain George Leigh-Mallory.
He was the guy who summed up the urge of the adventurer in a most pithy sentence.
Once when a journalist asked him why he wanted to climb Everest, he simply replied 'Because it's there!' No one has ever answered a question better! 'Because it's there' is now the rallying cry of all crazy adventurers all over the world.
Mallory was already known as one of the finest climbers in the world and he would make a bold bid for the summit. They had a devil of a job finding the mountain - and the weather went phut, ruling out any

question of making a climb at that time. But already 'Everest Mania' was on, and plans were being laid for a major expedition. Sir Francis Younghusband had retired and gone back to England, where he became Chairman of the expedition committee. A 'dream-team' of climbers and organisers was put together and they started on another attempt in 1922, with a small army of porters and mountaineers. They trekked 400 miles - all the way from Sikkim to Rongbuk monastery - just 15 miles from the North face of Everest. (now gone, alas. The Chinese Red Guards destroyed it during their brutal 'cultural revolution')

The first attempts were made without oxygen ('Only a rotter would use bottled oxygen' was a cheerful refrain of those days) and they managed to reach a most impressive height of 25000 feet. In further attempts, they managed to get up 27235 feet before being driven back. They had gotten within half a mile of the summit, and everyone was convinced it could be done.

They tried again and again - only to be thrown back. Once there was a great avalanche and a number of porters and sherpas died. Two climbers made it to 28126 feet - just 876 feet from the top - but just could not summit. Time was running out and soon the weather would make any more attempts impossible - so Mallory decided to make one last attempt alone with a young 22 year old climber called Irvine. They managed to reach the last camp at 26700 feet and decided to do the summit push the next day - June 8th - 1924.

But that was the last that the world heard of them. They vanished the next day and were never seen alive again.

Instead of Mallory claiming Everest - Everest had claimed Mallory.

## Phakding to Dingboche

That lodge which we had selected for being remote and empty had become so packed overnight that we left early morning without breakfast. It was already bedlam out there and waiting for breakfast to be served would have been futile.

And anyway I was nervous that they would discover that I was the one who finished off all the hot water and would come to beat me up.

Today was a big day for us - we would be formally entering into the Mount Everest area - the 'Sagarmatha national park'. The Nepalis got a bit indignant that their crown jewel is named after a bad tempered bushy bearded Anglo, and decided to call it by a local name. There already was a local name - Chomolungma - but the powers that be in Kathmandu (presumably) thought that this name was too Tibetan for their taste. So they conjured up a new sanskritised name out of thin air, and called it 'Sagarmatha' - which means 'Head of the sea'. Why a landlocked nation which is hundreds of miles from the coast and most of whose denizens have never even seen the sea (see what I did there? High five!) should call their mountain 'Sea-head' is completely beyond me.

But hey - nobody cares what I think - Sagarmatha it is.
(Though I am sure that if you catch a random Nepali and ask him 'What is Sagarmatha?' he will furrow his forehead - but if you ask him 'What is Everest?' - he will know instantly. Such is life…)

It was a lovely walk to Sagarmatha park gate, and the mountain claimed an offering from us when a gust of wind carried off Bharathi's cap when she was crossing a suspension bridge. I assuaged her feelings by laughing loud and long and pointing fingers at her and telling everyone else on the trail about it and making them laugh too.

I had a surreal experience at the gate when a local Nepali dude in typical Nepali dress asked us where we were from, and when I answered 'Bombay', his eyes lit up and he started speaking to me in fluent Marathi!
I was shocked! I thought I was hearing things and was going totally insane with the strain of travelling with Bharathi!

But no. It turned out that he had lived in Bombay for many years and had learnt the local language and was excited at the chance of speaking it again. Whew. I was not insane. What a relief.

From the gate it was a long steep climb to the village of Namche Bazaar, where we had to pay the entry fee to the National park. The fee at that time was a thousand bucks - but because we were Indians, we had to pay only a hundred rupees! WooHoo! I sneered at all the white guys and flashed my receipt at them. Suckers! Ha!

After a week of walking in rustic villages, Namche Bazaar felt like Vegas!

There was coffee! There was pizza! There was chocolate cake! There was steak!

After so many days of eating virtuous daal bhaat, this was like paradise for my mouth. We set to with a vengeance and ate and drank with abandon and nearly orgasmed with 'ooohs' and 'aaaahs' - much to the amusement of all the Johnny-come-latelies who had flown down to Lukla directly from Kathmandu.

'Wait you buggers' I thought 'Your time will come!' They would also be like this by the time they returned to Namche Bazaar.

There was even a department store! Bharathi went and bought all kinds of sensible things which we would need for the trek - while I went and bought a bottle of Tabasco sauce. The food was so bland that I thought I would pep it with Tabasco. (It didn't work, btw)

When we got back to the hotel, Bharathi turned to me with shining eyes.
'See what I bought!'
'What?'
'A chess set!'
I paled and blanched. 'What?! Why?'
'So that we can play of course! We will have something to do in the evening.'
'No no no….please no…not that again…'
'SHUT UP AND SET UP THE BOARD! I HAVE SPOKEN! I MUST BEAT YOU!'

Again I was able to distract her by requesting her to tell the story of her adventures - now we were in Cambodia.
The story of Cambodia started itself with high adventure - a day of high drama, extortion, frayed nerves and absolute helplessness . It was a 'sorta legal, sorta illegal' crossing into Cambodia from Laos at that point, because the legal crossing involved a 600 km, 5 day long detour via Thailand and no one wanted to do that. This

quicker and less legal crossing involved a lot of adventure and dollar denominated bribes to the Lao and Cambodia Immigration police mafia, and the boat mafia for the 50km trip down the Mekong. There was a lot of negotiation and bargaining on the amount of bribe money involved - Bharathi played the 'asian' and 'poor little woman' card, and then the whole group of 7 people banded together and asked for a group discount - the police in their turn cribbed that such a large party was unmanageable and involved extra effort, the local mafiosi demanded 'protection money' (only 17 USD, but backpackers go a bit crazy in Asia. And anyway - if you look too happy about low rates, then they might think that you have a lot of money and try to loot you physically)

Anyway - the 50 km Mekong ride was a tense affair, with no one knowing what was going to befall them! The narrow channels separated by lush jungles made them sitting ducks for bandits - but the bandits apparently knew that Bharathi was with them, and so ran for the hills! The party made into Cambodia without a hitch!

The main attraction in Cambodia is obviously Angkor Wat in Siem Riep, and she made it there after an epic journey consisting of a boat ride and a 14 hour taxi ride. Angkor Wat is obviously an amazing experience - though overcast skies robbed them of the epic sunrise over the temples shot. The temple experience of angkor is beyond belief - the sheer scale and vision of that architecture is mind boggling. It is the worlds largest Hindu temple complex - and it is interesting to note that most people in India have no idea about it!

From Angkor, she went to Phnom Penh - an 11 hour journey through amazing scenery and terrible roads. The country went through a wholesale rape by the communist armies of Pol Pot and his 'Khmer Rouge' ( 'Red Khmers') and they killed off about half the country - all the intellectuals, artisans, educated people and religious people. With all the two million landmines in the country waiting to explode in your face, nobody goes behind bushes here to answer nature's calls - you make do by the side of the road, well - limbs are more important than modesty! Even jeans-clad Khmer women carry along a sarong for this purpose.

Phnom Penh was a fascinating capital at the confluence of the Mekong and the Tonle Saap rivers - royal palaces and horrendous traffic, silver pagodas and begging landmine victims, spectacular sunsets and genocide museums - a tale of two cities indeed.

She had a most remarkable and harrowing adventure at the end of her Cambodian sojourn - she wanted to exit overland from Cambodia to Thailand, and sweated through a whole day to get to the border point due to the transport mafia's time wasting extortion dramas. They reached the border at 1645 hrs and had to scramble as both the borders closed at 1700 hrs. She got herself stamped out of Cambodia - and had the shock of her life when she found that as of 5 weeks ago, Indians were no longer allowed to cross into Thailand by land! The only way to enter Thailand was to go back to Phnom Penh and get a Thai Visa.

But how? Her Cambodian visa was a single-entry visa and she had been stamped out.

It was a traveller's nightmare - stamped out of Cambodia, and Thailand won't let her enter. She was stranded in the no man's land between two countries at 1730hrs standing between two locked border fences, with a hill to my left and the sea to her right!

Luckily, this being Asia, things were fluid. A small 'gift' of 5 dollars and an hours worth of negotiation enabled her to get back inside Cambodia and to get her departure stamp cancelled. She was back in Cambodia and was no longer a stateless refugee. She made her way back to Phnom Penh and went to the Thai embassy - only to be advised that Indian nationals on a tourist visa in Cambodia won't be issued overland visas to Thailand. The only way she could get a Thai visa is to fly from Phnom Penh to Bangkok and get a visa on arrival at Bangkok airport.

She screamed and fulminated at them, and they hid beneath their desks and pleaded that their hands were tied due to rules and would she please please please not shout at them boo hoo hoo. She was tempted to ditch Thailand altogether and go to Vietnam instead - but then decided that Thailand was the best option and she should not miss out on it just due to idiocy of immigration rules. So she caught a flight to Bangkok and exited Cambodia - with enduring memories of the mighty Mekong!

She landed in Thailand and got that blessed VoA and then decided to wash the asceticism of Cambodia out of her soul by chilling out in the beautiful and tourist-friendly beaches of Thailand. She went to famous islands of Koh Samui and Kohen's Phangan and chilled out in the beach resorts -she slept in a hammock right next to the beach,  one of those places on earth where a watch and calendar are meaningless. Koh Samui is famous for being the venue of the famous 'Full moon' parties - but not being a party animal, she gave them a wide berth. After that she switched coasts and went to Phuket - and voted the food there as being the best in the country, with Bangkok coming a close second.

A yacht owner's ad caught her eye - He was looking for passengers, four people max,  for an Indian Ocean voyage  of 6-10months taking in Andamans, India, Mauritius,  Seychelles, RSA and  off to Brazil.  Participants to bear expenses at actuals on the trip. Oh boy - what a temptation. But she had no money left. But that ad really tingled her soul, and she swore that she would do such a trip some day. Inshallah!

With only a week left in Thailand, she explored the famous 'James bond rocks' at the Phang Nga bay and did beach-hopping in Krabi, before looping back to Bangkok for mundane things like air-ticket reconfirmations.

Soon it was back to the Bangkok backpacker hostel, where she read an intriguing article in a magazine. It was titled 'Paradise can be boring' and went like this

… 'Resting in peace, we spend our lives seeking this - stretching out on inflatable mattresses, kicking back on a plastic recliner, sipping from a mini-bucket of Saeng Som and Red Bull with coke – escaping the apparently futile struggle of eking out a meagre living while ensuring an adequate supply of essential hi-tech toys, stopping ourselves from telling the boss to go to hell, swinging like Tarzan from paycheck to paycheck. Everyone hates it!

But after a couple of weeks of not kicking against the pricks, a horrible notion comes to light – Paradise can be dull. We are built to confront adversity, to interact and be stimulated. Living death, tempting as it is, is not for us.'

An interesting thought. Are we hardwired to get screwed? Is being happy just a mirage to be chased?

She had spent 930 dollars and 79days and 11 rolls of film in her South East Asian sojourn, and was left with 'one last crisp 100dollar bill, a few bahts, riels, kips, and many fantastic memories - Thilawsu roaring down, the Live Laugh Love go-go girls in Pattaya, never boring Bangkok, Mekong in Laos, kayaking in Nam Xang, Luang Prabang's charm, Vientiane's riverfront sunsets, the truly awesome Angkor Wat, the crumbling ruins of Kep, Ko Pha Ngan's Bottle beach, Krabi's Rai-Leh, all those interesting people who inspired, the kind ones who touched my soul, monks shopping in a IT plaza, a baby on a moving moped pillion rider's lap getting a IV drip from a bottle hanging down a bamboo pole, the sights, the smells, the sounds and emotions of an amazing land. After a trip like this, your life can never be the same again!'

And then it was back to Calcutta - and a flight to Kathmandu to meet me and start of a whole new adventure!

The next morning we again went to that German bakery to have some more of that awesome coffee. The menu was really tempting and we had some awesome pizza for breakfast. Then we saw that he had popcorn as well, so we had awesome popcorn for breakfast. It was all so …er… awesome… that I wished that I could store it in a hump like a camel.

But now it was time to move out of that oasis and go back on to the trail. But we were sure we were coming back here on the way out.

We hit the road again, and the views were absolutely fantastic. Now we were inside the Sagarmatha area, and all the great peaks were on full display.

The immensity of the Himalayas is hard to envisage, because the scale is simply immense. The range is so wide, that if we imagine the most westerly of the peaks - Nanga Parbat (now in Pakistan) to be in London - then the most easterly peak - Namche Barwa (in Arunachal) would rise somewhere in Moscow! Or in other words - if the Himalayas were in the US, then they would stretch from New york to Houston, Texas!

And Nepal is at the heart of them - out of the 14 mountains in the world which are taller than 8000 meters, 8 of them are in Nepal. And how tall are those? If you put the Appalachian on top of the Rockies - they would still be shorter than the Himalayas. If you took the highest mountain in the Andes - Aconcagua - and put the tallest mountain in England - Ben Nevis - on top of it … Everest would still be 2000 meters taller than that.

And these were the mountains around us - we could see them! Everest, Lopche, Ama Dablam - they were all in sight!

I could hardly believe it. I was setting eyes on Everest! Me!

Sir Francis Younghusband had written 'Mount Everest for its size is a singularly shy and retiring mountain. It hides itself behind other mountains. On the North side, in Tibet, it does indeed stand up proudly and alone - a true monarch among mountains. But it stands in a very sparsely inhabited part of Tibet an very few people ever go to Tibet. From the Indian side only its tip appears amongst a mighty array of peaks which being nearer, look higher.'

Everest may not dominate the view like a lone star - but it rules the landscape like a king in a court full of noblemen. Even the noblemen are amazing to look upon.

I was in awe.

But awe or not, we had a long walk ahead of us - and it seemed to be almost entirely uphill!

We were headed to the village of Tengboche, which was at an altitude of 3860 meters. Yesterday we were at 2610 meters at Phakding, and that shows how much uphill we were going.

I was huffing and puffing my way up, when I was again passed by the Brad Pitt lookalike, looking very dapper in his French Legion style cap. Seriously, that guy must be causing all the Nepali women to go weak at the knees. We met a bunch of Indian trekkers for the first time in Nepal. They were a Bengali bunch from Calcutta, and were very impressed when they learnt that we had trekked all the way from Jiri - and also that there were just the two of us. Indians tend to travel in groups, and independent travellers are a bit of a rara avis.

We finally reached Tengboche, and checked into the 'Trekkers lodge'. Lodging was fairly scarce in Tengboche for some reason, and that lodge was very crowded. It was like staying on the road!

But what views! Tengboche has probably the best views on the EBC trail - being surrounded by massive snow-covered massifs. Everywhere you look, there is a legendary peak. It's like being in the biggest, grandest, most divine cathedral in the world! There is nothing quite like it.

Tawache, Everest, Nuptse, Lhotse, Ama Dablam, and Thamserku - all amazing peaks! Bharathi was in raptures, and pointed them out and named them to me like a Lama explaining the wheel of life to a disciple.

There is a huge monastery at Tengboche and we went to see that - it has a kickass location with an awesome backdrop of Ama Dablam. The monastery is the leading Buddhist centre in the Khumbu region with a residing Rinpoche who blesses pilgrims, mountaineers and travelers passing through. Everest expeditioners visit the monastery to light candles and seek the blessings of gods for good health and safe mountaineering.

Every October, Tengboche Monastery hosts the colourful Mani Rimdu festival, which is a culmination of Buddhist celebrations with a religious gathering, songs, ritual dances and enactments of the lives of legendary figures. The ancient monastery burnt down in a fire in 1989 - but it had been rebuilt since then. This monastery should consider itself lucky - it's sister monastery was the Rongbuk monastery on the other side of Everest - which was in Tibet, and was torn down stone and pebble by the crazy Chinese communists. Tengboche - being in Nepal - survived and is thriving.

Interestingly, Tenzing Norgay, the first man to reach the summit of Mount Everest with Sir Edmund Hillary, was born in the area in the village of Thani and was once sent to Tengboche Monastery to be a monk.

When we came back to the lodge, Bharathi again took out the chess set and demanded slaughter and pain - and was extremely happy when she won 5 games in a row!
'BUHAHAHA! I AM THE GREATEST! I AM THE CHAMPION! I AM THE MOST BEAUTIFUL!' she screamed and danced around the room.

Maybe it was the oxygen deprivation affecting my brain - but I thought she looked really cute when she was so happy.

The next morning, we woke up to those incredible views again! I pinched myself to see if I was dreaming - but no. I was very much awake and I was really living this awesome experience. The sacred mountain of Ama Dablam was actually smiling down on me! I was actually seeing Lhotse and Everest and Nuptse and all the rest. Crazy shit!

We had crossed the tree-line now and the countryside was all brown and sere. We were in the proper Tibetan plateau area - and there were no trees or grasses to be seen. But the earth itself had so many different colours - it was like a painter's palette.

People who fly into Lukla have to spend a day or two in Tengboche for acclimatisation - but since we had walked up from Jiri, Bharathi felt that we could press on ahead to Dingboche, where the accommodation scene would be better. There would be more options and there wouldn't be such a crush.

We set out, enjoying the excellent weather and the views. Ah, the views!

You know - while it is indeed great to see the great peaks of the world - I must say that for me, it was just as great to see the sky. What a sky! It was a brilliant blue… a cerulean blue, as the artists might say - and it was totally different from the sky we see in the cities. There was no pollution and we were so high up, and the sky seemed to be brighter, bluer, more luminous and bigger than any skies I had ever seen!

People would laugh at me, I thought - looking up at an empty sky rather than at the amazing mountains. But when I looked around, I saw a fair amount of people looking open mouthed at that sky. Big sky country indeed!

On the way we again met Paul - the American dude who was passing himself off as a Canadian. It turned out that he was here on work!
Work? Here? What kind of work?
He had apparently conned some university into giving him a grant to study ancient techniques of hill road building. What this meant in practicality was that he trekked for a living and occasionally took photos of roads and chatted with people on how they are made. What a sweet scam! It's right up there with studying the effects of orgasm denial on sex addicts, or a study on the best topping for pizzas or a rigorous investigation on which brand of beer is the tastiest.

We made our way to Dingboche village at a very respectable 4410 meters and got a room in a lovely lodge called 'The Snow Lion'. God knows where they think up these names…no lion has ever been seen in the snow ever. Why would Tibetans even know what a lion is anyway? They would know a snow leopard, or possibly a tiger - where would they ever have seen a lion? Very strange.

4410 meters is very high up, and though

the sun was out - the air was very cold indeed. The breeze just cuts through clothes and shoves an icy finger right up your bum and sniggers when you jump in fright. The Snow Lion guys had actually made a greenhouse in their yard. A cabin made of glass which let the guests enjoy the sun without getting their butts frozen off in the wind. There were a lot of people sitting inside and vegging out with a book.

That looked really enticing, and I also went inside and selected a book from the stack and sat there to read - but then it got too hot! The sun's heat got trapped inside and it soon became too uncomfortable for me, and I started gasping. But when I got out of the glass house for a breath of fresh air - I froze and shivered.

Gah.

I got irritated and went inside our room and saw Bharathi all snuggled up inside the blankets - but still complaining about the cold.

'I thought you sleep in tents pitched on snow when you do your mountaineering expeditions?' I said in wonder. 'What kind of fraud mountaineer are you anyway?'
'Oh shut up.' She grumbled. 'I am not on an expedition now, am I?'

I waggled my eyebrows at her and patted my bed.

'Come and join me in my bed then. We can share our body heat. That's an accepted mountaineering technique I believe.'

I didn't mean anything by this - it was just a polite flirtation. I had been too sore and sick (and shit scared of her, to be completely honest) to actually do any flirting till now - but now that I was acclimatised and fit, my natural gallantry just slipped out.

Imagine my surprise, when she screamed 'FINALLY! YES! YES! YES!' and leaped into my bed like a jackrabbit! She put her arms around me and hugged me and drew the blanket over us.

'EEEEEEK!' I was scared out of my wits! 'NO NO NO NO… I was just making a general remark...it was just a URGH!' I shut up as she clasped me around the neck.

'HELP! HELP!' I shouted

'SHUT UP AND HUG ME YOU FOOL' she growled

'Yes ma'm' I said automatically …and hugged her.

We lay twined together under that

blanket feeling that delicious warmth build up between us. We felt extremely cosy and languorous and totally relaxed. Every muscle in my body relaxed and I seemed to melt into a puddle. We lay like that for hours, just cuddled up.

'YOU ARE A REALLY SLOW FELLOW - BUT YOU SEEM TO BE GETTING THE IDEA NOW.' She growled at me.

'Yes ma'm.'

We had decided to stay in Dingboche for a day anyway - to acclimatise …so it turned out to be very convenient for us. We stayed cuddled up in bed till evening, getting handsy and acquainted - until hunger forced us down to the restaurant for dinner.

The next morning we were all lovey dovey and lazy in the morning and couldn't get up the gumption to leave the warm bed - and each other - to go out for our acclimatisation hike to nearby Chukung. We finally managed it, with great reluctance - but even mother nature cooperated with us by sending down some bad weather and driving us back into the lodge.

Then it was back into the cosy bed for us, as we moved on to necking and smooching and general handsiness. This trek was turning out far better than I thought! WooHoo!

Romance on the mountain, baby!

It turned out that Bharathi had been bowled over by my radiant beauty and had fallen in lust when she first me in my shitty office, and this whole EBC trek was a long drawn seduction process to get me into the sack. I mean - most lovers use chocolates and flowers and stuff like that - but only Bharathi can think of using a Himalayan trek as a seduction mechanism!

'YOU ARE MINE NOW! BUHAHAHAH!' she crowed at me 'I ALWAYS WANTED A BOY TOY!'

'Er…what?!'

'SHUT UP AND KISS ME!'

'Yes ma'm.'

**Dingboche to Lobuche**

Now that we were sharing a bed, it was an even bigger wrench to leave that lovely warm cocoon - but up we must get, as Winston Churchill might have said.

(Obscure joke - apparently once an editor objected to a dangling participle in his writing and an enraged Churchill wrote back - 'This is the kind of arrant pedantry, up with which I will not put!')

(No? Didn't get it? Not funny?…oh well…)

We hit the road and set out for Lobuche - the next stop. The scenery was all Himalayan desert now - brown mountains, stony paths, blue skies and of course - majestic snow-clad summits. The 'roof of the world' just above the tree line - and it is quite amazing how the greenery vanishes. No trees, no shrubs, no grass - inspite of having ample water. The Tibetan plateau is dry and almost moon-like. But the thought struck me that it was not all one colour - Oh no. There were innumerable shades of brown and earth colours - like the palette of an impressionist painter. Every rock, every strata, every plain seemed to be of a different colour - and these would also change with the light conditions. Every colour would look different in direct sun, under clouds and shadow, at different times of the day. It was if Mother Earth wanted to compete with Mother Nature and show that you can have spectacular colours even without any living creatures.

The colours ranged from the brilliant white of the fresh-snow clad peaks, to the bluish white of the ice, to the dirtier colour of the old snow, to the almost soil-like colour of the ancient glaciers - which in turn were dotted with bright blue and white colours of the fissures and avalanches and crevasses. Then you had the black stones and cliffs, the granular colour of the moraine and loose boulders, then a whole range of colours of the soil itself...it was mind-boggling.

And of course, there was the amazing range of colours of the sky - the blushing pink of the morning, the brilliant blue of the clear day - and a whole range of blues as it got windy, dusty or overcast - culminating with the brooding dangerous grey of bad weather. You had a whole different range of colours of clouds - the white puffy pillow-like cumulous clouds, the long trails of cirrus clouds, the dark cumulonimbus ones - and a whole range of clouds whose names were unknown even to the most eminent of meteorologists!

And don't forget the waters! They ranged from the brilliant blue of the glacial lakes, to the white rushing waters of the fast-moving rivers, to the muddy brown of the slow-moving rivers and wet-lands, the tiny flashing rivulets and waterfalls…

Bharathi kept pointing out the various summits and telling me anecdotes about them - this mountain was first climbed in this year by that person, and the saddle of Ama Dablam is something or the other which has slipped my memory, and something about the approach to Pumori which was something that would interest only a nutty mountaineer, and how Lhotse is blablabla and Nuptse is totally different - it is blublublu…

Whatever. She was babbling away and I was just letting it wash over my ears and nodding and grunting.

(This technique turned out to be so useful that I am still using it 18 years later. )

Her enthusiasm and joy in the surroundings was enough for me to enjoy.

In fact she was bubbling over so much that various people on the trail also warmed to her and we chatted with a number of different trekkers and guides.

Earlier we were just two weird people on the trail - a bald clueless fellow and a tiny wolverine-like creature who terrified everyone. But now that we were behaving like a couple, we were suddenly popular. 'She has not killed this bald buffoon yet, so it must be safe to talk to her' is what they must have been thinking. And in my case 'I wonder how long he will survive - let me chat with him in the time he has left - poor fellow)

We had become famous on the trail as the 'Chess players' - and people who I wouldn't know from Adam (and Eve, I suppose) would smirk at me and ask - 'So… who won yesterday?'. This was OK when Bharathi had won, because she would smirk and say 'Me! ME! ME, OF COURSE! BUAHAHAHA!' and do a little dance - but if she had lost, then she would go as dark and dangerous as the most forbidding cumulonimbus and grumble about cheaters, and hypoxia, and I didn't mean to do that but he wouldn't allow me to take back a move which I had made ten moves earlier - HE IS SUCH A MEANIE! I AM GOING TO KILL HIM! - And scare off the questioner completely.

We were also popular with the guides - as we had common ground in being Hindi-speaking, fellow 'Asiatics' as the colonials might say…and in Bharathi's case - having a profound interest in mountains!

She would first look at the guide with narrowed eyes and quiz him to see whether he was a worthy guide and worth talking to, or a fraud to be ruthlessly exposed! She would pepper him with questions

TELL ME THE NAME OF THE 14 8000ERS!

HOW MANY ARE IN NEPAL?

HOW MANY CAN I SEE FROM HERE? WHICH DID I SEE YESTERDAY? WHICH WILL I SEE TOMORROW?

HOW DO YOU TIE A CLOVE-HITCH KNOT?

WHO CLIMBED NUPTSE FIRST? SECOND?

And so on and so forth.

The guide would go pale and start sweating with fear and some of them would go insane and throw themselves off the mountain rather than face SHE WHO MUST BE OBEYED! Even today the slopes of Everest must be lined with gibbering lunatics - guides who went out of their senses with fear.

Even the Abominable Snowman ran away and hid in Tibet - preferring to face the Red Army rather than face Bharathi.

'Here' I said, whispering in her ear 'Stop scaring away all the guides. If all of them go insane and run off the cliff then who will escort these poor trekkers back home?'

I used to comfort them by talking about Bollywood movies and TV shows and politics and hot women and then they would feel a little better. It must have been a strain on them also to be interacting only with the firangs and talk in a language you are not totally familiar with and smile all the time - and it must have relaxed them to speak in their own language and interact with people who were just passers-by and not paying customers. We would have a chat and possibly laugh at a joke, and maybe - just maybe, they would roll their eyes at the unreasonable behaviour of a guest. But mostly they were too professional for that.

Apart from the mountains and the sky and all that, the other unsung wonder of Nepal is - the people! The mountain people are so friendly and cheerful and polite and gentlemanly and always ready to smile and laugh a bit. Their faces have a thousand lines - a testament to the harshness of the sun and wind and cold - but when they smile, their whole face lights up.

And they are incredibly strong and fit! The porters look like small thin guys whom you wouldn't suspect of superhuman strength in the least - but they carry loads weighing more than themselves and carry them for days and days and miles and miles over the most steep mountains. I used to be in awe, seeing them in action. They were like human ants - being able to carry many times their own weight - fed only on a simple diet of daal bhaat and potatoes.

The potato planting done by the surveyors and pandits had had great results, and it was now an essential part of local food. I would be sitting and chatting with the porters, when suddenly someone will bring a hot steaming plateful of tiny boiled potatoes with a very tiny dip of spicy chutney, and announce 'Come brothers! Let us eat potato!' and they would polish off that plateful happily. They would always invite me to join them, but I would always demur. They clearly needed the calories more than I did.

The Tibetan people (and these are all of Tibetan stock) apparently used to be a fearsome and warlike race in the past - but when Buddhism took hold here with its message of gentle submission and avoidance of bad karma - it totally changed their national character. They became a gentle and friendly people (you don't want to mess with them though - a hillmans fury is a terrible thing) One should travel to the Himalayas just to meet and interact with these wonderful people and see those wonderful smiles.

We reached Lobuche after a 5 hour walk, and found that there were only a few lodges there, and all the rooms were sold out. We had only dormitory beds available ! I was most downcast - but perked up when I saw that they had privacy curtains around the beds. WooHoo!

Lobuche was at an eye-watering elevation of 4910 meters, and it became very cold very soon! We needed no more motivation and jumped straight into bed and crawled into the blankets and cuddled up. (To share body heat! Hypothermia can be terrible!) I spent an instructive evening finding out what could make Bharathi squeal out loud - especially as she was all embarrassed about being in a dormitory and wanted to remain silent at all costs. It was an exercise in self control for her, and a worthy challenge for me and my wandering hands.

While I was lying all warm and comfortable in my bed, my mind went back to the Everest story and how things were not so comfortable for Tibet.

After Mallory's death in 1924, the mountaineering world took a step back, so to speak - and there were no major expeditions. One of the reasons why Everest expeditions came to a hard stop was a rather strange story, which became famous as 'The affair of the dancing lamas'.

Mallory's death became a very big deal in the UK - his memorial service was attended by Royalty, and Mallory became famous as a martyr to mountaineering. (One wonders if he would have been as famous if he had actually succeeded). The expedition photographer -John Noel - made a film about the expedition called 'The Epic of Everest' - which was a big success. Unfortunately for him, the very success of his film sealed the fate of future expeditions.

To promote this film, he invited a team of Tibetan monks to tour the west and put on shows of chanting and ritual dances in the movie theatres before the films - and this was where the trouble began. The Dalai Lama was outraged at the film and dance routine , which he felt was a mockery of Tibetan religion - and there was a scene in the film which particularly offended them. It showed a guy de-lousing a child - picking out the lice from the scalp one by one…and eating them! Like a monkey!

The Dalai Lama was so offended that he banned all mountaineering expeditions altogether. The monks were recalled to Tibet and severely punished (and severe punishment in Tibet was no joke - it could involve whipping, blinding, hands getting chopped off and execution) and all expeditions were stopped! It was a huge embarrassment to the Everest committee and Sir Francis Yoounghusband and became a diplomatic issue between the countries.

There was a strong subtext to this - as there was a tussle going on between the theocratic government of the Dalai Lama and the generals of the Tibetan army, who wanted western help to upgrade the army and the guns and ammo and stuff. The Dalai Lama felt that the Army was gaining too much power, and he used this outrage as a convenient excuse to emasculate the powers of the generals. He claimed that this film was somehow the fault of the generals and carried out a putsch and curtailed the powers of the army. This turned out to be a very unfortunate thing to do - as all this weakened the army and kept it at a medieval technology level, and hence they were not able to defend Tibet from the invasion of the Chinese army in 1950.

The 'Affair of the dancing Lamas' thus had very wide and very long range repercussions.

The immediate upshot of all this was that there were no more mountain climbing expeditions to Everest via Tibet- But there was a most interesting expedition to do an aerial reconnaissance of Everest from above - a very great challenge in those days of primitive planes and unpressurised cabins. It was one of the last great and audacious adventures involving Everest.

The pilot was a guy with a very long name - Air Commodore Douglas-Hamilton, 14th Duke of Hamilton and 11th Duke of Brandon, KT, GCVO, AFC, PC, DL, FRCSE, FRGS - who was a most powerful personality. He was the son of the Duke of Hamilton, and was educated at Eton and Oxford and became a Boxing 'Blue' for Balliol college, Oxford - (indeed, he went on the win the Scottish amateur middleweight title in Boxing) and also represented the college in rowing! (He was known as the 'Marquess of Douglas and Clydesdale' and must have learnt boxing just to beat up people laughing at him for having such a silly-sounding title.)

He became interested in flying from a young age and joined the Royal Auxillary Air Force in 1927 and after rapid promotions, became the youngest Squadron leader in the RauxAF. Since he was a senior pilot - and a rich nobleman to boot (by now he was 'Lord Clydesdale') - he was a perfect candidate for an audacious plan thought up for seeing the summit of Everest.

It was called the 'Houston - Mount Everest flight expedition' and the idea was that they would fly above Mt Everest and do an aerial reconnaissance and see the world's highest mountain from above! A very great challenge for the primitive aeroplanes of the day! No one had ever flown so high before.

The expedition was named for - and sponsored by - Lady Houston - a most fascinating lady. She was a British philanthropist, political activist, and suffragette and an aviation enthusiast and pioneer - and an owner of a newspaper! She was known as the 'Saviour of the Spitfire'. She donated £100,000 (some £3.4 million in today's money) to keep research going into the Spitfire's predecessor – the

Supermarine S6, a single-engined racing seaplane – when Ramsay MacDonald's Socialist government pulled funding for the project during the Great Depression in 1931.

Lady Houston was aghast at the cutback in defence preparedness of the country under the Socialists, and basically said 'Fuck you' to the government and paid for the engine R&D out of her own pocket.

In fact, in 1932 she had offered to give 200,000 pounds to strengthen the British Army and Navy. The British government refused the offer - and so, she hung a huge electric sign reading 'DOWN WITH MACDONALD THE TRAITOR' in the rigging of her ship and sailed around Great Britain!

She sent them a telegram - a very prophetic one as it turned out - 'I alone have dared to point out the dire need for air defence of London. You have muzzled others who have deplored this shameful neglect. You have treated my patriotic gesture with a contempt such as no other government would have been guilty of toward a patriot.'

Anyway - With her support, the Supermarine company developed the Supermarine engine and actually won the coveted 'Shneider trophy' - an international race for seaplanes and flying boats.

Without the help from Lady Houston, Britain would not have gained the experience in producing high-speed aircraft - and it was this technical experience that led to the development of the Spitfire fighter, just in time to join the Royal Air Force in fighting off the Luftwaffe in 1940 in the Battle of Britain and saved the UK from German invasion after Dunkirk.

If not for Lady Houston, the UK would have definitely lost the Second World War, and you might have been reading this book in German!

So who was this Lady Houston? Its a fascinating story - like a romance novel! 'Poppy Houston' came up from extremely humble origins - She was a Chorus girl ! - and at the tender age of 16 she attracted the wealthy – and married – brewer Frederick Gretton of the Bass family and they eloped to Paris. This was her first introduction into high society and you can just imagine the guts and gumption of the plebeian daughter of a humble box-maker to assimilate into the upper class. She managed to become a part of the swish set - and she got married for the second time in 1901 to George Frederick William Byron,

9th Baron Byron of Rochdale - who had no money, but made her a Baroness! In 1924 she got married for the third time - she married another baronet, Sir Robert Paterson Houston, a ruthless Liverpool shipowner and Conservative MP whom she nevertheless got the better of. He once showed her his will, bequeathing her £1 million. She is said to have torn it in half, declaring: 'If I'm only worth a million, then I'm worth nothing at all!'. A million pounds! In the 1920s! An ex-chorus girl! Amazing!

Old Houston ended up leaving her more than 6 million when he kicked the bucket - leaving her one of the richest women in England, and the owner of a newspaper and a fancy yacht, among other things. She became a firebrand in that conservative society - taking on the government, supporting the Suffragette movement ( which was among the first women's liberation movements in the world and got women the right to vote in the UK) and became a supporter of new technology and of aviation.

As one of the richest - and most audacious - supporters of aviation, she was approached by Lt Colonel Stewart Blacker, who wanted to organise the world's highest flight - over Mt Everest itself!

(Lt Col. Blacker has an interesting connection to our story - he was a descendant of Valentine Blacker - ex Surveyor General of India, and contributor to the Great Trigonometrical Survey of India which I referred to earlier. Valentine Blacker was considered the other great personality in the Survey after Everest himself. )

Lt Col. Stewart Blacker was a British Army Officer and weapon inventor - he invented the 'Blacker Bombard', a precursor of modern anti-submarine and anti-tank weapons. He was a fighter pilot in WWI and was shot down several times. After retirement he had married well - to the daughter of an Earl - and was doing very well as a weapons inventor. Think of him as an early-day Tony Stark. (I am Iron Man)

As a mix of Army officer, flyer, inventor and empire-builder - he wanted to carry out some audacious project - something full of adventure, something never done before - something which would impress the natives and show them the power of the 'pucca sahib' and kill the brewing Indian Independence movement and save the empire.

All of these were hot buttons for the magnificent Lady Houston as well, and she agreed to finance this daredevil mission and signed a cheque for 15000 smackers!

The flyers decided to use the highest-end planes of the day - special 'Westland' planes with modified engines - and transported them by sea to Karachi (now in Pakistan) , and then to Purnea, now in West Bengal, India.

These were simple bi-planes with propellor engines and unpressurised cabins - the mind boggles at the courage of these pilots who would pilot these fragile contraptions to such rarified heights!

And they did! The Houston - Mt Everest flight expedition was a complete success!

What a photo! This was the first time that human beings saw Everest from above.

The photographer damaged his air hose

during the first ascent and fainted briefly from Hypoxia before waking up and repairing it! This flight proved the need for specialised equipment for high altitude flights - pressurised cabins, heated clothing, oxygen supplies etc - and made modern jet flight possible.

The first attempt couldn't take photos due to dust - but the second attempt produced usable photos - The airplanes carried fancy survey cameras that would take photographs of the surface at specific intervals as the airplanes flew over known survey locations. It was planned that a photographic mosaic of the terrain and an accurate map could be drawn. It was a huge revolution in aerial photography!

These photos proved very valuable to Hillary and Tenzing in planning the first successful submitting of Everest several years later.

For this achievement of flying above Everest and successfully capturing it on film, Air Commodore…er…Lord Clydesdale…er…his grace, the Duke of Hamilton…ah, whatever you want to call him - was awarded the Air Force Cross. What a dude!

As 'The Guardian' said in 1933 - 'It is a splendid achievement - not for any material gains, any additions to aeronautical knowledge that it brings, for it brings few or none, but simply because it was one of the few last great spectacular flights in aviation which remained to be done.'

Check out this link for an awesome set

of photos of this adventure - https://mashable.com/2016/10/01/flying-over-everest/#0xfTJNzwMsqE

This was the last happy and inspiring news on the Everest front for many years, unfortunately.

WWII broke out after this, and all the flyers in the world were engrossed in other things for many years. All the great mountaineers were either fighting in the wars or were summarily banned from doing any climbing.

One the great German mountaineers - Heinrich Harrer - was arrested in British India while planning an expedition to climb Nanga Parbat (now in Pakistan - then in British India), and had to do a quite extra-ordinary escape to avoid being jailed in an internment camp for the duration of the war. He managed to escape into Tibet and spent time in Lhasa and became a tutor to the current Dalai Lama - a story told in his fine book 'Seven years in Tibet'. The book was later made into a movie starring Brad Pitt.

The earlier Dalai Lama had had his horoscope read, and it said that he - and his country - faced great trouble from foreigners, and so they closed the borders and banned all Europeans from entering Tibet, earning it the sobriquet of 'The Forbidden City'.

However, it turned out to be a totally different foreigner who was going to cause great trouble. After WWII, Mao Tse Tung managed to win the Chinese civil war and throw out the Nationalist armies of Chiang Kai Shek. Now he had a large battle-hardened army and no money. He noticed that Tibet had a lot of money (due to its gold mines and other mines) and lacked a large battle-hardened army.

It didn't do a genius to do the math.

Mao claimed the fig leaf that Tibet used to be a part of China in the days of the Ming emperors, and so it should be part of China now as well. The Red Army attacked Tibet and in a matter of months, occupied the country entirely. The Tibetan army had only ancient muskets, and the monks had only curses to fight with - and both proved ineffective against the modern ammunition and brutality of the Chinese. And boy - were they brutal! They killed and murdered and tore down monasteries and temples and burnt holy texts and generally made a huge mess of the place.

The Dalai Lama had to flee to India to save his life and Tibet fell - the Chinese swiftly put up a 'Bamboo wall' and cut off all contacts with the outside world. No foreigner was allowed to enter Tibet and no Tibetan was allowed to leave it.

The Tibet route to Mount Everest was firmly closed!

**The top of the world**

We left our dorm bed behind in Lobuche and set out for the final stop!

Ooh - I was so excited! We were going to Gorakshep, which would be the last and highest staying point of the Everest Base Camp trail, and at almost 5000 meters, it was very high indeed! We would stay in Gorakshep overnight and then make a dash for the actual base camp the next morning and come back to Gorakshep.

Woo Hoo.

We had a late start from Lobuche - part of it was the high altitude, part was the reluctance to get out of bed - and we slowly and happily trudged up to Gorakshep. There was no hurry at all - we had all the time in the world. We walked slowly, looking at the amazing beauty around us and trying to soak in the memories like a sponge might soak up water.

It was fun bumping into the same guys again and again - you just look at them in the first bump, then you graduate to a nod, then it becomes a friendly smile, then a few words, then some information and factual exchange, then laughing and joking - and the best part when you are comfortable enough to pull each others leg and poke fun. In some cases, one never really goes beyond the nodding part though you might be meeting for years and years - and in some cases you leapfrog through the phases and go to the laughing and pulling legs very fast indeed.

Me? I never pull anyones leg. Ever. Oh no.

We met all kinds of people - a tyre-selling dude from the US who marvelled that everything was so cheap here, some aggressive German climbers who introduced themselves to the locals saying 'You are a sherpa from Nepal, we are Sherpas from Bavaria!', a honeymooning couple from Russia…the lady was so good-looking, like a Dresden doll, that I quite lost my heart to her. The guy was also very handsome in a 'teenage dream' kind of way - they looked like they had come from central casting of a Russian romantic movie! They had been quite non-plussed to find themselves in a dormitory last night. There was a Danish driving instructor who had spent almost a year backpacking around India (the joys of earning in a strong currency and spending in a weak one), there was a group of elderly Japanese trekkers who really impressed me by their walking discipline and song singing - though I felt that their guide was a bit of a supercilious bully, there was a European group who were on a very expensive managed trek...it was like a United Nations up there. A United Nations the way it should be - everyone happy and cheerful, making efforts towards a common goal, living amicably and having a good time.

A lot of people were on organised treks, and thus were accompanied by guides and porters to carry lots of lots of luggage - tents, kitchen, food, supplies, chairs, tables, and also their backpacks! All these guys had to carry were a small daypack which would hold their water and cameras and personal stuff. Even the hard-up Russian couple had a guide who carried their backpacks for them - the sight of that skinny guy carrying three backpacks and outpacing all of us was most humbling.

When we chatted, they would curiously ask us where were our porters and guides, and Bharathi would bristle at them and ask them why on earth they needed a guide on such a well defined trail, and why did they need tents and supplies when there were so many tea houses and why they couldn't carry their own backpacks? They would blench and hide in corners as SHE got into full cry and started haranguing them about how SHE used to carry all her stuff on her own while trekking in India.

'I CARRIED ALL MY STUFF! I CARRIED THE COOKING EQUIPMENT! I CARRIED THE SUPPLIES! I EVEN CARRIED THE PORTER! SOMETIMES I EVEN CARRIED THE HORSE!' SHE would scream away, and this would continue until I tugged her by the elbow and …er…carried her away as she got …er…carried away!

'Has she gone?' a whisper would come from the nooks and crannies, and when I replied in the affirmative, there would be sighs of relief from various hiding places and the firangs would slowly emerge, wiping their brows and looking cautiously around.

We found a room at Gorakshep in a very cramped lodge. It had the smallest and most uncomfortable beds ever - but hey… getting a bed and blankets at 5000 meters is itself a great blessing. You didn't need to carry sleeping bags and tents and stuff, and you weren't freezing your tits off in the cold outside - it was a place to count your blessings.

It was too high and cold a place to build a proper toilet and plumbing - so the toilet situation was primitive. A large ditch. It had a wooden plank to sit on, and a tent to cover your bare bum from the elements. Oh well - it's not that you spent a lot of time there anyway.

The hotel had a cosy dining lounge, where we sat and played chess - yes, that had become our daily evening pastime. (I had to intentionally lose to keep her in good temper…but don't tell her that, OK? It will be our little secret.). There were very few tea houses at this altitude - and interior space was limited. But it was freaking cold outside and only Canadians and Siberians would dare to go outside, so all the hikers would be packed into a tiny space, like sardines in a heated can. If you wanted to pee in the night, you would walk over half a dozen hikers and their groans and squeals would wake up everybody in the place.

The thin air and cold kept everyone a bit quiet - but there was a frisson of excitement in all of us. We would be at the Base Camp tomorrow!

As we slept off in that Gorakshep lodge, so close to the end of the trail -  my thoughts went back to the beginning of this Nepal trail - in the 1950s!

Before the war, all the Everest

expeditions had been through Tibet - but now that road was closed due to the Chinese invasion. The Tibetans were entirely screwed, poor sods - but an important side-effect of the Chinese invasion of Tibet was that Nepal suddenly opened up to foreigners.

    Earlier they had been all snooty and stand-offish, not wanting to see a single westerner inside their country. But after they saw what happened to their neighbour across the fence, they got shit-scared, thinking that it might be next on the Chinese invasion list! So they decided that it was time to reopen relations with the Western powers and make new friends as a counter-balance to China, and allow foreigners to enter their country for mountaineering.

For over one hundred years Nepal, ruled by the Rana dynasty, had not allowed explorers or mountaineers into the country. However the country was in ferment after 1947 - when the locals saw that India had become free and was enjoying freedom and democracy. The Rana regime was seen as being despotic and cruel and there was a popular uprising against it - and it soon became vicious after the entry of the Nepali Maoist parties into the revolt - and Nepal suspected that China might be supporting these Maoists with money and ammunition.

A possible communist-sponsored revolution was even less welcome than Western influence so Nepal opened diplomatic discussions with the United States. In 1950 Nepal gave permission for the French Annapurna expedition and Annapurna I became the first eight-thousander summit to be climbed, under the leadership of the eminent mountaineer Maurice Herzog. Herzog wrote a book about this - 'Annapurna'. (It is a great read, but some people sniffed that there was more Herzog in it than Annapurna.)

The British Joint Himalayan Committee, successor to the Mount Everest Committee, was then given permission for an expedition to explore the region north of Annapurna – Annapurna IV, Manaslu and Himalchuli – at the same time as the French attempt on the mountain itself.

The eminent mountaineer Bill Tilman was the head of the expedition and he grasped the opportunity to scope out a southern route to Everest. He assembled a team of Sherpas and explorers and they trekked up what was to become the Everest Base Camp trail - up the Dudhkosi to Namche Bazaar, which was a prosperous village due to its trading links with Tibet over the Nangpa la pass. From there they went to Tengboche, where they were warmly received at the monastery. From there they looked around for a passage, but couldn't find anything until they ascended Kala Patthar and took a vital photograph - which showed a possible path to Everest.

We would be going to that historic point tomorrow - Kala Patthar, here we come!

The more dedicated of people got up at 3 AM and set out in the bitter cold to see the sunrise from the viewpoint of Kala Patthar - but Bharathi utterly refused to do this.
'Get out of bed at this hour? ARE YOU MAD? SHUT UP AND LET ME SLEEP!'
'But the others are all leaving…' I whined. 'I can see them - going off to catch the sunrise.'
'THE PLACE WILL LOOK THE SAME, SUNRISE OR NOON!'
'But…'
'GRRRRRR!'

SHE finally deigned to wake up and we set out for the final push! It was cold and the air was thin and the trail was very steep and difficult, but the thought of reaching the pinnacle of the trail filled us with enthusiasm

It was a wonderful day, and we did the fairly difficult two-hour climb to Kala Patthar

...and we were there!

WE WERE THERE!

WE WERE THERE!

WE WERE THERE!

WOOHOO!

We could see everything clearly - the black and rocky summit of Everest, the Khumbu icefall, the glacier, the tents of the actual Everest Base Camp - where I suppose the actual mountaineers were shaking their heads and smiling at the bumbling amateurs of the trekkers looking down at them.

We were at the spot where Tilman took that photo! We were where Hillary and Tenzing might have stood and looked thoughtfully up at the mountain.

WE WERE AT 5545 METERS!

I and Bharathi linked arms and danced around and kissed and slapped each other on the back. How crazy was this? A guy who had never ever done a Himalayan trek was at the top point of the Everest Base Camp trek. In fact, we were overlooking the

Base Camp, so we were even higher than them. The Base Camp is at 5364 meters, while we were 200 meters higher. We could see the tents and the piles of supplies and the tiny figures of the mountaineers and support staff puttering around.

All that climbing, all that sweating, and gasping, and huffing and puffing - all that effort had finally brought us to this! The culmination! The entire Everest range lay in front of us - we would see the Khumbu glacier, the dangerous ice fall, the Nuptse ridge… and the black and rocky massif of Chomolungma herself! The mother goddess smiled down at us. It was a picture perfect day - clear, and sunny and just perfect.

I just sat there and soaked in the feeling. What a sight. We were truly at the feet of the gods.

I was feeling very fit and proud of myself, until I saw the Swiss group arriving and smiled to myself. We had been bumping into that group regularly, and had become friends with the oldest member of the group. He was 75 years old!

Let me repeat that - 75 years old!

All my thoughts of being very fit

evaporated as I saw that 75 year old gentleman climb up and give us a broad smile. I was not fit - he was fit! What an inspirational figure.

We shook hands and he shared out Swiss chocolates as a celebration and we sat and chatted for a bit. This was not the end of their trek - they would be crossing the Cho la pass and going to see the glacial lakes of Gokyo and then descending to Namche and Lukla.

We sat there for about half an hour and then started to go down.

We had done it.

No, let me shout it out…

WE HAD DONE IT!

WE HAD DONE IT!

WE HAD DONE IT!

Woo…gasp…hoo…gasp…huff…puff…

We had done it!

Back in the past, the race was heating up in the mountaineering world as who would win the laurels for the first ascent of Everest. Nepal was handing out only one permit per year - so opportunities were very limited and had to be grasped.

In 1952, the Swiss Mount Everest expedition set a new elevation record - reaching a height of 8595 meters - but were not able to summit.

The next chance went to the British expedition of 1953 - and it was a crucial opportunity, because the French had received permission for 1954 and the Swiss for 1955 and so the British would not have another opportunity till 1956. A lot can happen in that time - so as far as the Joint Himalayan Committee of the Alpine Club and the Royal Geographical Society was concerned, it was now or never!

Colonel John Hunt of the British army was selected as the leader of the expedition, and this caused a lot of murmurs, because everyone expected the eminent and experienced mountaineer Eric Shipton to be appointed. Shipton was extremely experienced and had done the reconnoissance expedition earlier and was very familiar with the terrain. But he was known for his preference of small and agile expeditions, rather than giant military-style campaigns with huge amounts of people and equipment. He was also considered as 'NOT having a killer instinct' - which many people felt was a good thing. Killer instincts get people…killed.

But the Joint Himalayan Committee did not agree - they had only one shot at this, as their next slot was after 3 years - and a lot can happen in three years. They had the money, or were confident that they could raise it, and so they wanted the highest possible chance of success - which meant mounting a very large-scale campaign…the very thing that Shipton was against. So they appointed the ex-army man Col. Hunt to the job instead - something that rankled with all the climbers in the party.

But Hunt was a good guy and managed to win over the hearts of all the members - which included a certain bee-keeper from New Zealand - a Mr. Edmund Hillary. The team included 13 other climbers, a couple of doctors, photographers etc - and they hired a bunch of elite Sherpa climbers and guides as well. The British members of the team came over by ship - which Hunt preferred as the long voyage would enable the members to relax and get to know each other well. The kiwis came by air.

The team was hosted in Nepal in the British embassy, as there were no hotels in Kathmandu at the time. (Which sounds so strange today - when there seem to be more hotels than private residences in Kathmandu. Just shows you how much things can change)

The Sherpas chosen for the trip came to Kathmandu to help carry loads to the Western Cwm (no, that's not a spelling mistake. A cwm means 'a steep-sided hollow at the head of a valley or on a mountainside'; and is of course a Welsh word - because the Welsh seem to hate vowels with a passion) - and were led by their Sirdar - a certain Mr Tenzing Norgay, who would be making his 6$^{th}$ attempt at Everest. He had done the last trip with the Swiss team and liked them a lot. He was reluctant to join the British team at first, but was finally persuaded to lead the Sherpa team as the Sirdar.

The expedition almost got off to a bad start, due to the casual racism of the British staff. While the white climbers and Tenzing the Sirdar were given rooms to stay in , the porters were not allowed rooms or bedding, but were told to sleep on the floor in the garage! They were not given any toilet facilities either - so they got up and pissed en masse in front of the Embassy in protest at the lack of respect shown to them. Fuck you all. The expedition almost got cancelled before it began - but then there was a lot of explanations and apologies, and things went forward as planned. Hunt must have shat bricks out there!

Things got sorted out, and they trekked without any further incident along the same EBC trail which we had walked on till Tengboche, where they waited to get acclimatised. Then they went on to the base camp and set up the assault. And it was truly an assault! They had a party of 350 porters, 20 guides and tonnes and tonnes of equipment and a number of experienced climbers.

Hunt planned for three assaults of two climbers each - they needed to finish before the monsoons, or they would have to wind up and come back after the rains. The pilots established a route through the Khumbu icefall, and then the sherpas moved tonnes of equipment to the advanced camps. Camp 2 was established at 5900 meters, camp 3 at 6200 meters, camp 4 at 6400 meters, camp 5 at 6700 m, camp 6 at 7000m at Lhotse face, and camp 7 at 7300 m - and finally they reached the South col at 7900 meters.

These numbers may sound small - but every inch was hard fought for! Even the first step of finding a safe route through that ice fall on the Khumbu glacier was extremely difficult and dangerous, as it was prone to frequent avalanches and cracks and fissures. All the climbers had to tie ropes to each other so that they could be saved if one guy broke through the ice and fell into a crevasse. Some of these crevasses were so deep, that you couldn't even see the bottom! A solo guy faced certain death if he fell into one of these. The mountain was utterly unforgiving - as they knew very well…the memory of Mallory was with them all the time.

Hillary himself fell into a bottomless crevasse, and was saved only by the swift action of Tenzing, who jammed his ice axe into the snow and managed to anchor them both and prevent them all from going inside. This was the beginning of the relationship of absolute trust between the two on the mountain.

Setting up the camps was extremely hard work, as the advance party had to climb up, find a suitable spot, go back down to collect the tents, go back up to pitch the tents and mark out the camp, and then the team had to make a number of trips to ferry equipment up and cache it and set up a camp. Even climbing up after the camps were set was a monumental effort - the climbers had to go up to acclimatise, then climb down to sleep at a lower altitude, then climb up again the next day - then climb down again to base camp. They had to do this up-and-down a number of times to ensure that the body acclimatises to the high altitude. The bones would create more red blood cells, the lungs would get used to extracting oxygen from the thin air, and the brain would literally rewire itself to make the body survive. The whole process of climbing from base camp to last camp would take a minimum of two months of extreme effort - after the camps had been set up!

It took the effort of more than 350 men and several tonnes of material to make the camps and enable the attempts. Just think of the pressures on the head of the expedition to manage all this stuff - in a foreign country, in such harsh terrain. There was no civilisation north of Tengboche monastery in those days, apart from a view itinerant yak herders - and their supply chains ranged all the way from Namche Bazaar. Anything you wanted had to be planned way in advance - as the process of acquisition was so long winded.

Now it was time to make the summit attempt! The first attempt was done by Tom Bourdillon and Charles Evans - and they reached within 100 meters of the summit before having to turn back!

So close! Dammit!

The second attempt was done on 27th May 1953 - by Edmund Hillary and Tenzing Norgay. Norgay had previously ascended to a record high point on Everest as a member of the Swiss expedition of 1952.

Well, there is no mystery here…you know the story! THEY DID IT! THEY DID IT!

They left their cold and windy tent in camp 9 at 6.30 AM (they had planned to leave earlier - but Hillary's boots had frozen solid, and they had to wait for two hours for Hillary to thaw them out.) They set out towards the peak and climbed up the Nuptse ridge. At the end of it, they saw a huge mass of snow and ice, which would be very easy to clamber over in the plains - but at this altitude, it looked quite impossible. But Hillary studied it minutely, and thought that he could figure out a way to ascend it using ice axes and advanced climbing techniques. This idea proved successful - and that stretch came to be known as the

'Hillary step'. It is the last great obstacle to climbing to the top. Once they crossed it - they saw that there was nothing more to climb. They were at the top.

They reached the South Summit at 9 AM, and reached the summit on 29th May 1953!

Everest had finally allowed humans to come on top.

They stayed for about 10 minutes, Hillary took a photo of Tenzing at the summit - and in a rather astounding show of modesty, declined to take any photo of himself! They left offerings on top as a thank offering to Chomolungma - a silver cross and some chocolates, and then descended.

Neil Armstrong famously said that thing about 'A small step for man, a giant step for mankind' when he stepped on the moon. Hillary, being a laconic Kiwi, did not stop to think up any pithy memorable words. What he said was 'Well George…we knocked the bastard off.'

Not exactly the words to be written in gold - hence you have probably not heard of it.

When they came down, it was the biggest news in the world! The correspondent on the spot - James Morris of the 'Times' - was so paranoid about other newspapers stealing his news and printing the news first - that he sent a coded message by runner to Namche Bazaar. The message read 'Snow conditions bad stop advanced base abandoned yesterday stop awaiting improvement' - just in case some other unscrupulous hack had bribed the telegraph operator.

The code was correctly deciphered in London, and the Times printed a wildly successful exclusive about the successful summiting of Everest by the British expedition! The rather inconvenient news that the actual summiteers were not English - one was a New Zealander and one a Nepali/Indian - seemed to have been conveniently ignored.

The news broke on the day of Queen Elizabeth II's coronation - and the wildly jubilant British public treated it like a coronation present. The honours flowed in thick and fast - Hillary had already been appointed a Knight Commander of the Order of British Empire and Hunt a Knight Bachelor before they came down the hill! Tenzing could not be awarded a Knighthood as he was not a UK citizen - so he was awarded the George medal - the highest award for civilian gallantry.

The Government of Nepal presented Tenzing with a purse of ten thousand rupees, which was then about £500. Hillary and Hunt were given kukris in jewelled sheaths, while the other members received jewelled caskets. The same day, the Government of India announced the creation of a new Gold Medal, an award for civilian gallantry modelled on the George Medal, of which Hunt, Hillary and Tenzing would be the first recipients.

Further honours continued to descend on the members of the expedition: the Hubbard Medal of the National Geographic Society, which had never before been awarded on a team basis, although individual medals were struck in bronze for Hunt, Hillary and Tenzing; the Cullum Geographical Medal of the American Geographical Society, the Founder's Medal of the Royal Geographical Society; the Lawrence Medal of the Royal Central Asian Society; and honorary degrees from the universities of Aberdeen, Durham, and London.In the New Year Honours list of 1954, George Lowe was appointed a Commander of the Order of the British Empire for his membership of the expedition.

Shipton laconically commented on the successful ascent: 'Thank goodness. Now we can get on with some proper climbing.'

Nobody gave me a medal - but I got a nice kiss from Bharathi. Given her high standards, that was a signal honour indeed!

## More adventure! Chola pass and Gokyo

After spending those triumphant minutes at Kala Patthar ( 'Kala patthar' that means just 'Black rock' - btw. The guy who named it was really literal and had no creativity in his bosom) we descended back to Gorakshep and celebrated with some hot lemon tea and relaxed for a bit, and then picked up our packs and started descending down. The trek was over - our destination had been achieved, and now it was just a return down the paths we had already trodden.

For some reason, this really irked me... after so many days of breaking new ground and something for the first time every single day, the thought of walking back on trails already trod (is that a word?) was not appealing.

As Bilbo Baggins said

Upon the hearth the fire is red,
Beneath the roof there is a bed;
But not yet weary are our feet,
Still round the corner we may meet
A sudden tree or standing stone
That none have seen but we alone.

I wanted to see more - trek new roads,

see new things. My time with Bharathi had just begun - was it to get over so soon - just when my feet have hardened and my stamina has gone up and my body acclimatised? What a pity.

It was a relief to walk downhill again after so many days of climbing upward and onward - But that soon felt boring and unfamiliar. Where was the challenge? Where was the feeling of my lungs burning, my legs complaining?

And of course, the thought kept playing in my mind that once the trek was over…my magical time with Bharathi would also be over.

I would go back to Bombay and to my office and my daily commute and idiot bosses.

Bharathi was still on her sabbatical, and would end up god knows where. Was this one of those 'two logs floated together for some time in the ocean and then drifted their separate ways' situation? Would we also part ways - forever? How do I handle this? How do I process this? What the fuck do I do? I had never done this before.

I didn't even want to think about it for

now. I want to live in the moment. I want this moment to last forever. Well…at least I want it to go for some time more. Me, her, the mountains, the trek, the adventure, the togetherness…

Both of us were silent on the way down, and we bumped into our Swiss friends again at Dzongla. The 75 year old dude and his group. We said 'Hi' and stopped to chat and after some time we said Bye - or rather, 'Au revoir' - ' We shall meet again' - because no doubt we will keep bumping into each other on the trail.

No no, the old man smiled at us - our paths part here. We are going to Gokyo and then coming down to Namche by a different path - so we may not meet again.

'Gokyo?' I said. 'What's that?' I had only heard of Tokyo.

Gokyo, it turned out, was a village on the other side of the mountain, which was famous for having some beautiful glacial lakes. You had to cross a high snow covered pass called Cho la pass and cross the Ngozumpa glacier - the longest glacier in Nepal - and it was quite a difficult crossing. You would need ropes and special equipment to come down the pass. This group was a full service trek with guides and porters and stuff, and the sherpas would be laying down fixed ropes for the group to come down by. We had nothing except torn and bald old sneakers - and each other.

Oh I see - I said, and shook hands and wished them well and me and Bharathi carried on.

For a few steps.

Then we stopped.

Come on…this 75 year old man is going there…we can also go. How can we leave adventure behind ? I also want to see the blue lakes of Gokyo.

'It's a snow covered cliff!' Bharathi said.
'Yes.' I agreed 'And we don't have proper gear…I mean, look my shoes…these are torn ancient Power Joggers. They should not have been used for mountain trekking, let alone in snow.'
'True.' Bharathi also agreed. 'And we don't have any ropes or crampons or ice axes or even a stick.'

'Tampons?' I was confused. Why would I need women's sanitary doodads?

'Not Tampons, idiot. Crampons.'
'We will get cramps?'
'GRRRR.' Bharathi growled at me. 'Not cramps! CRAMPONS! Those shoes with metal pointy soles which enable you to get a good grip on icy slopes! Ignoramus. Idiot.'
'Ah. OK. I see. But …why are they called crampons?'
'ARRGHH! Never mind the etymology! We just don't have any!'
'No Etymology? OUCH!' she had kicked me on the shin.

'And we have no money.'
'It's a very bad idea.'
'Terrible idea.'
'Stupidity.'
'Utter Stupidity.'
'We have done what we set out to do. Now we should quietly go back to Namche Bazaar.'
'Yes. Pizza and cappuccino is calling.'

We walked a few more steps. But very slowly.
'It would be a silly thing to do.'
'Very silly.'

'But we shall go!' Bharathi announced.
'We shall?' I was stunned. 'But we just agreed it was a silly idea. We have no tampons'

'Crampons!'
'Yes. That.'
'I DON'T CARE! I CANNOT STAND BY AND WALK AWAY WHILE AN OLD OLD FART DOES THE CLIMB AND WE DONT!'

'Er…we cannot stand by and walk away at the same time…that's two different things…'

'SHUT UP!'
'Yes Ma'm.'
'WE ARE GOING!'
'Yes ma'm.'
''LET'S GO!'

She turned around and flounced back, and I ran after her.

"Forward, the Light Brigade!"
Was there a man dismayed?
Not though the soldier knew
  Someone had blundered.
  Theirs not to make reply,
  Theirs not to reason why,
  Theirs but to do and die.
Into the valley of Death
  Rode the six hundred.

Boldly they rode and well,
Into the jaws of Death,
Into the mouth of hell
  Rode the six hundred.

We met the amused Swiss team again, and said 'See…the correct thing to say was 'Au revoir' after all' and we walked up towards Dzongla village, and enjoyed fine views of the Cho la lake.

But when we approached the pass, I stopped and gulped a bit.

It was a vast slope of virgin white snow! And it seemed to go on for ever! I felt like Hillary looking at the Khumbu ice fall for the first time and biting his lip and wondering if this was really a good idea? Wouldn't it be better to go back home and get bitten by a 100 bees everyday than this?

We were going to climb up that? In sneakers? I hadn't no experience of snow at all - in Bombay we are more into torrential rains and flooding. You show me a raging Amazon river and I would yawn a bit and be unmoved. But snow and ice I had only seen from afar. I must have ingested more snow and ice in my drinks than I ever stepped on.

But I could feel the glare of SHE WHO MUST BE OBEYED burning blisters on the back of my neck, and so I took a step forward into that white stuff.

'Shit. Shit. Shit' I mumbled and stepped

into it and screamed 'EEEEK' as my foot went inside and the snow went inside my sneakers. Bloody hell!

I went sploosh sploosh sploosh as I trudged through the snow and Bharathi yelled out to me 'NO NO NO …YOU ARE WRONG!'
Eh? What did I do?
'When walking in snow, you should walk like this.' She declaimed like a drill instructor. She splayed her arms out and waddled her backside like a mama duck trying to teach the butt-ugly duckling something. 'The main thing is to maintain your balance! If you are unbalanced, then you will slip and fall.'
'But you are already unbalanced…' I muttered, and quailed as she glared at me.
'SHUT UP!'
'Yes ma'm!' She had screamed so loudly that all the sherpas also froze and stood still in shock.
'PAY ATTENTION!'
'Yes ma'm!' the whole mountainside focussed their attention her.
'I WILL SHOW HOW TO WALK ON SNOW!'
'Yes ma'm.' I looked around, and saw that all those mountain-born-and-bred sherpas were also standing stock-still and ready for instruction.

'You plant your heel in first and then put your weight on that leg ...ARE YOU PAYING ATTENTION OR NOT, YOU MISERABLE WORM?...and then take another step, like this....EEEEEK....' She went SLIRRRR ....as her back foot slipped on the snow and THUMP as she fell butt-first into the snow.

Then she yelled 'EEEEEK EEEEEK EEEEEK' like the mating call of some exotic bird.

I was watching her with interest. This must be some new technique, I thought. Buttwalking, or something like that, so have maximum traction on the snows.

'Is the screaming part of the technique?' I asked with interest 'Like some sort of chant or something? Does it give you spiritual power? Is that how the weight-lifters scream while lifting a heavy weight, or the karate and Judo boys scream while kicking and boxing?'

'OH SHUT UP AND HELP ME UP! THE SNOW HAS GONE INTO MY BUTT CRACK!'

I stomped through the snow and went and helped her up.

'Upsy-daisy!' I said, brushing her off and spending a long time patting her butt...to get the snow off, of course.

'I WAS STILL RIGHT!'

'Yes…of course, of course…' I said, still patting away.

'I WAS RIGHT AND YOU WERE WRONG.'

'No doubt…no doubt…'

'YOU WERE JUST LUCKY.'

'True..true…'

'Are you done feeling me up?'

'In some time…'

We managed to get to the top of that snow-covered hill and stopped. What a glorious view! Wow! That was just fantastic! A fantastic panorama of snow-covered peaks, with a humongous river of ice below us. That was our first view of the mighty Ngozumpa glacier. What an amazing sight!

This was the longest glacier in Nepal and it looked very imposing indeed. The ice was clearly very ancient - as there was no such dirt and soil settled on it that it looked brown in colour. But here and there, it was riven by cracks and fissures and you could see the white and blue of the virgin ice.

But then I looked down! And I gulped again and again!

Shit! We were on top of the pass and looking straight down!

It was a sheer bloody cliff!

We were facing a steep drop - I felt like I was on top of El Capitan in Yosemite and looking down! I gulped as I saw that drop. We have to go down that? How? I would need Gandalf the Grey to call the great eagles - Gwaihir the windlord and Landroval - to get me down from here.
(I know I know, I am a huge LOTR nerd.)

'This is the end! I am done for! We are going to die! Tell my parents I loved them! Kiss me, Hardy!' I moaned. But there was no help for it - we had to go down somehow. I moved slowly towards that cliff - but then I heard the guide of the Swiss group call out to me.

'Hey brother - here, come here.'
I went to him, and he showed me the fixed rope they had...er...fixed...
'Use this...hold the rope and go down carefully.'
'I say! Thanks a lot! But haven't you fixed it for your group ?' I said
He smiled and patted my back. 'Arre ... the rope is there...use it...don't worry about it.'
That was so nice of him! I was touched. He must have charged the group a good bit

of money for the rope, and here he was offering it to us for free. I wrung his hand and thanked him, but he just smiled and brushed it off.

We came down that snow slope holding on to that rope, like a clumsy spider descending from his web for the first time - and when we reached the bottom I sighed with relief! Without that rope, there was no way we could have come down. Safely, that is. We would have come down, but very fast indeed.

I would have rolled down like Captain Haddock in that Tintin comic and made a huge snowball of myself before falling down into the depths. I wiped my freely streaming brow as we finished the rope descent and landed on the rocks.

Later we met a guy who had been watching us come down - and he had watched in horror, fulling expecting us to do a high dive and go splat into the ground.

'That was freaking dangerous.' He scolded us. 'Never do that again.'

I folded my hands and nodded. Never again, without the adequate precautions. The patron saint of idiots is with us, but we should not strain the poor guy too much.

The challenge was not yet over - now

we were facing a whole slope of glacial moraine - gigantic boulders and stones pushed down by the glacier. We had to hop from boulder to boulder like monkeys till we crossed that moraine. I gasped with relief when we came to end of it - I was soaked with sweat inspite of the cold and snow.

BUT WE HAD DONE IT! WE HAD CROSSED CHO LA PASS!

We had crossed the Ngozumpa glacier - the longest glacier in the Himalayas. It comes down from Cho Oyu and is 36 kilometres long, and were rewarded by the sight of the first of the famous Gokyo lakes. The lake looked so amazing - it was a wonderful deep blue in colour and looked like the eye of some giant magical creature - a blue-eyed dragon or something. We were so happy to see this lake and as a reward for having done the Cho la descent safely, we just sat there together for some time and took in the beauty of the place.

There are a number of lakes in Gokyo, and they are supposed to be holy to both Hindus and Buddhists. People actually take a ritual dip in these lakes during a religious festival in August. Brrr. The very thought of stripping off and entering the lake caused me to shudder and shrivel up.

We made our way to Gokyo village and celebrated with a hot lemon tea!

'Here's to idiocy!' I cried.
'Lunacy forever' she replied, and we clinked our cups.

We found a nice hotel in Gokyo and chilled out there, and greeted a number of people who we had met on the trail - the honeymooning Russians, the 'Sherpa from Bavaria' Germans, the Italians etc.

The next day we trekked up to the local high point - Gokyo Ri at 5357 meters! It was a rather irritating trek, as it was full of false summits…you get very happy at thinking that the slog is over and you have reached - but no! You have to keep walking. Ah, we have reached! No! Keep walking, sucker!

But finally when we got up there, it was worth all the trouble! What a view!

Wow!

It provided a 360 degree view of the magnificent landscape and you can see all the great peaks standing in front of you -the 8000ers Mount Everest, Lhotse, Makalu, and Cho Oyu, the other grand peaks of

Lhotse, Nuptse, Nang pa, Gyachung and Makalu- and also the amazing Gokyo lakes!

Amazing! Mind boggling! Awe-inspiring! Too good!

This would be last high point we would visit, so we sat there for a long time soaking the views in and greeting all the guys we had met before as they all came up one by one and gasped at that majestic sight.

I was really glad we had succumbed to the call of adventure and done this.

We came down feeling as happy as Hillary and Tenzing must have felt while coming down from Everest.

I read up on both these guys later, and was fascinated by them.

Hillary was a huge tall guy - 6'2" or thereabouts, and it was amusing to read that he was a tiny fellow in school and was bullied around - he learnt boxing to increase his self confidence! His family was into bee-keeping - they had 1600 hives to take care of, and probably got bitten every day.

My mind …buzzed…with all kinds of puns about this!

He would certainly know about the bees, if not about the birds.

'Hi honey' must have been a confusing greeting in his house.

'Getting a buzz on' would have a different connotation here.

He would invite his guests over 'for a bite'

If he had allergies from bee bites, would he get 'hives'?

Was he really as busy as a bee?
Did he tell people to buzz off?
Did guests ring the buzzer?

(OK OK, I will stop now…)

Maybe he took up mountain climbing just to get away from the bees! He started climbing at 16 - and discovered that NZ is a great place for mountaineering. He tramped all over the Waitakere ranges and sumitted Mt Cook or 'Aoraki' as it is called in Maori. (Aoraki means 'cloud piercer' and I thought that it was a lovely name for mountain that can be seen poking through the clouds.)

After climbing Everest, he also went to the South and North poles - and thus was the only person to have done the 'Three poles'. He even went for an expedition to find the Yeti - and, unsurprisingly, he …er… didn't. He got a lot of honours from a lot of governments - but perhaps the most interesting one was that he was featured on a New Zealand 5 dollar bill - making him the only living person not a current head of state ever to appear on a New Zealand banknote! He insisted that the mountain in the background be the NZ mountain and not Everest.

Tenzing Norgay's was also a very interesting story. As he said about his journey - 'It has been a long road ... From a mountain coolie, a bearer of loads, to a wearer of a coat with rows of medals who is carried about in planes and worries about income tax.'

Tenzing was born to a poor mountain family and his parents thought of making him a monk and enrolled him in Tengboche monastery! But he decided that this life is not for him and ran away to Kathmandu and later to Darjeeling, where he started out as a porter in expeditions. Norgay received his first opportunity as a 20 year old to join an Everest expedition when he was employed by Eric Shipton, leader of the 1935 British Mount Everest reconnaissance expedition. He became well known in mountaineering circles and was involved in several attempts on Everest before his big success with Hillary.

After that historic feat he became an international celebrity and was heaped with a number of awards and honours - The UK government gave him the George medal, the Nepal government gave him the Star of Nepal, the Indian government gave him the Padma Bhushan and appointed him the first Director of Field Training of the Himalayan Mountaineering Institute in Darjeeling, when it was set up in 1954.

He was also selected by the Kingdom of Bhutan to conduct the first ever trek for foreigners in Bhutan. The official trek began in Paro, northern Bhutan and included a visit to Tiger's Nest (Paro Taktsang), the ancient Buddhist monastery, before returning to India via Nepal and Sikkim. Norgay even introduced his group to the King of Sikkim (the last king of Sikkim, as Sikkim is now a part of India) and also brought them to his home in India for a farewell celebration.

But the most interesting honour for him was that a mountain range was named for him - on the planet Pluto!

Tenzing Montes is the name of an icy mountain range on the surface of Pluto!

## The end of the trek - Namche, Lukla

Now the unplanned adventure was also over, and it was time to start the return journey. But we would be returning to Namche Bazaar by a different route - so it would still be a new trails for us and we wouldn't have to retrace our steps.

We were in no hurry now, and had a lazy morning cuddled up under the warm blankets and started walking only by 8.30. We took a last look at those amazing Gokyo lakes and drank in that azure blue (We didn't actually drink it…that would be silly. We drank it in with our eyes. Duh!) and crossed the meltwater stream of the Ngozumpa glacier. It was downhill all the way to Machermo - a cute village in the valley.

It was most pleasant as we walked down the roads - the sun was warm and comforting, and the breeze was chilled and soothing, and the views were …you know it dude…they were awesome. And it was very nice to be walking in good company. Me and Bharathi were sharing a very pleasant vibe, and it was not just an erotic haze or anything. We were just clicking together and having a free flow of conversation and thought process.

We had a good mix in having enough things in common to have a sense of familiarity - we were both MBAs and had experience of working in Indian corporates. We had even worked for the same company - though we didn't know each other at the time. We were both avid readers, and shared a rather twisted sense of humour.

But at the same time, we were so different. I liked movies and music - and she was almost mohammedan in her ascetic refusal to see them. She was a rolling stone - having lived in hostels and many cities, while I had lived in Bombay all my life. She didn't drink or smoke, while I did both. She was into crazy adventure and travel - and I was just taking baby steps in that direction.

And of course she was a complete and utter nutcase.

I had to scratch my head on that one… was that a commonality or a difference between us? Hmmmmm.

It was so beautiful that we decided to stop for a hot lemon tea. The proprietor was a most ordinary looking guy with a couple days worth of beard and beer breath. He was happy to see Indians - a rare sight perhaps - and we chatted for some time in Hindi, talking of this and that.

Our talk drifted - understandably - to mountains and mountaineering…and SHE was babbling away as usual about the various peaks, and soon the proprietor also joined in and mentioned some points as well. This really tickled SHE, and they chatted away companionably babbling about mountains and expeditions and stuff.

I then told that guy about Bharathi's credentials. She is a student of the two major mountaineering colleges in India - I said - she has done advanced mountaineering courses in the Nehru Institute of Mountaineering and the Himalayan Mountaineering Institute.

'Really?' his eyes lit up. 'That's great! Do you know mumbledname Sherpa who was an instructor there at such and such time?'
'Yes! Yes I do' Bharathi replied and they had a short conversation about mumbledname.
'How do you know him?' She asked
'Oh we are friends' he replied 'We did a bit of climbing together.'
'Oh really? You climb?' Bharathi asked, all set to dispense her pearls of opinion and advice about climbing.

'Oh I climb a bit.' He said very humbly.
'Where all have you climbed?' she asked - and gasped as she heard his answer.

This unremarkable looking guy with beer breath and three days growth of beard turned out to be a mountaineer...an elite mountaineer! He had summitted Everest! And Cho Oyu! And Ama Dablam! He showed us his photos and certificates.

Amazing. Most impressive.

Bharathi nearly pissed herself with excitement! She looked like a groupie who has just discovered that the guy in front of her is the drummer of her favourite band. She squealed with delight and clapped her hands and jumped up and down and giggled.

(Well, she didn't...but it is fun to imagine it)

Just shows how little you can tell (OK OK...how little I can tell) about a person from his looks. Still waters run deep. I wondered how many of the folks wandering about and chilling in the streets around here would turn out to be legendary mountaineers. Here I suppose that just existing and staying alive in the winters and monsoons would take a high amount of mountaineering, snow walking and ice walking capability. The whole place must be freezing solid and getting covered in tonnes and tonnes of snow in the winters.

I remembered a passage from Heinrich Harrer's '7 years in Tibet' where he describes a scene where they - elite mountaineers - come to a high pass with a waterfall flowing over it and decide that it is too steep and dangerous to climb at night and then see a local Yak herder drive his entire herd of yaks over that steep waterfall pass before clambering over it himself, barefoot. What we think is superhuman, is frequently just a boring commute or chore for the locals.

We continued descending down to Dole village, and my body was so tuned to descending that the smallest ascent had it shouting 'Are you fucking kidding me?!!' and leaving me gasping. I discovered that descending can be really hard on the knees - and my knee was complaining loudly!

We spent the night in Dole in a very cute little hotel, and then left the next day for Namche Bazaar. We had crossed below the tree line now, and it was seriously weird to see green trees all over the trail after so many days of bare brown views. The trail to Namche is not a consistent downhill, but a rather irritating up and down trail where you climb up hills and down dale and up hill and down dale and up… Oh all right…you get the idea.

It took hours and hours to reach Namche Bazaar and I was soaked in sweat and totally fagged out and my knee felt like it was on fire! And my instep wasn't feeling too good either. I was drooping like a wet sock, as Wodehouse might say.

But no matter! I changed out of my sweaty clothes and slathered that fiery Tiger balm on my knee - for we had a very important task to do. Very important! Most Urgent! A Matter of life and death! It could brook no delay!

We had to eat cake!

We hit that bakery like starving people and ate everything in sight!
We had chocolate cake! Apple pie! Pizza! Coffee! More Coffee!

Ah! What bliss! Especially after all those days of daal baat. I had tried livening things up with splashes of Tabasco sauce - but that experience had been a total failure.

Even Tabasco cannot save these dishes.

But eating that moist gooey chocolatey cake was worth all that trouble. The psychologists talk glibly about 'delayed gratification' - but they should observe this to see a real life example of it in action. When you put that heavenly chunk of calories in your mouth , after days and days of tea-house fare - it is like an orgasm in your mouth! You drool, your eyes close of their own accord, you see stars and moan uncontrollably.
'OOOH OOOH AAAH…YES, THATS IT….RIGHT THERE…..OOOOH…..AAAAAH'
Sex is all fine, but chocolate cake after doing the EBC - now that's really something.

Then you have the pizza - heavenly hot steaming pizza - with a lake of melted cheese covering mountains of salami and ham and onions and herbs…oh…oh my. You sprinkle some chilli flakes and oregano on it, and break off a triangle, looking reverently at the long strings of cheese extending from the slice to the plate - and then you put it in your mouth…

BLISS.

Ah ah ah….starburst…oral orgasm…
OOOOOOOOOOOHHhhhh….

All the flavours merge together as you chew, and your saliva mixes with it all and creates a whole new flavour and even swallowing that is a sensorial pleasure. You will go back for a second slice, and a third - but nothing can match that joy of that first bite and that first slice.

 made it through the wilderness
Somehow I made it through
Didn't know how lost I was
Until I found you

I was beat
Incomplete
I'd been had, I was sad and blue
But you made me feel
Yeah, you made me feel
Shiny and new

Hoo, like a virgin
Touched for the very first time

You're so fine
And you're mine
Whoa
Whoa, ah
Whoa
You're so fine

And you're mine

Eh? Whats that? Why did we have cake first, and then a pizza?

Oh that's easy…we had cake while we were waiting for the pizza to be made…and then we had more cake after the pizza.

Then we had coffee! Actual cappuccino, from a machine.

And then I saw that they had popcorn on the menu.

Popcorn! Really? I immediately ordered it, and were gobsmacked when she brought out an enormous plate of fresh hot popcorn. I am not normally a fan of popcorn, but at that time it seemed to be a dish fit for the gods themselves. Me and Bharathi closed our eyes and drooled all the crisp and crunchy stuff and inhaled that lovely salty aroma. I cannot describe adequately what a sensorial rush that was. Incredible! Amazeballs!

Sated and satisfied (does that mean the same thing?), we staggered back to the hotel and crashed on the bed. We were physically, mentally and emotionally spent.

We had done it.
We had completed the EBC.
We had eaten the popcorn.

The next day was the actual and final last day of walking. But before we started walking we went back to that bakery and had popcorn for breakfast, much to the amusement of everybody there.
We went down to Phakding - I started out by limping and cursing a good deal due to my complaining knee, but then I took a pain killer pill and once it kicked in, we went jumping and prancing down and singing with excitement.

We kept bumping into various people we had met so many times on the trail and we shared happy smiles and nods and the occasional chat. It was a most lovely day - with the full complement of blue sky, white clouds, warm sun and a gentle breeze . It was a very nice send off. We felt really sad bidding farewell to our friends - the mountains which had been our constant companions for so many days…Thamserku, Kangka, Everest, Nuptse, Khumbila…

After lunch at Phakding, we had to hurry up a bit as we wanted to hit Lukla before dark. My knee said 'Hey! Watch it mister!' and I had to placate it with another shot of pain killers.

We managed to reach Lukla before dusk and checked into the fancy 'Sherpa lodge'. The lodge was so fancy that it had its own very fancy hot shower facility - a magnificent sauna and jacuzzi and powerful showers with unlimited hot water!

I was moved to tears! A hot shower! Unlimited hot water! Oh Joy! Bilbo's bath song flowed out of me.

> Sing hey! for the bath at close of day
> That washes the weary mud away!
> A loon is he that will not sing:
> O! Water Hot is a noble thing!
>
> O! Sweet is the sound of falling rain,
>   and the brook that leaps from hill to plain;
>   but better than rain or rippling streams
>   is Water Hot that smokes and steams.

Our only earlier experience of a shower on the trail was a very interesting bucket shower at a lodge. You pay for a bucket of hot water and then go and strip off and stand in the bathroom naked and shivering and shrivelled up, wondering where is the bloody hot water ? There was no spigot to turn or handle to pull.

Then the lodge guy comes trudging up, carrying a bucket of hot water from the wood-fired boiler, climbs up a ladder to the top of the shower cabin and pours the water on top of the startled bather who screams with shock! EEEEK! The hot water is poured into a container on top of the cabin and it showers down on the waiting bather through the …er…shower …and you have to frantically soap up and rinse off before the water runs out, else you will have to shout out to the lodge guy and wait there wet and freezing until he comes back with another steaming bucket.

To see this gleaming pipework emitting unlimited amounts of electrically-heated water was like a sight of god itself! And that was only the shower! There was a magnificent wood-lined sauna which would have looked at home in the finest of spas, and a jacuzzi with jets of hot water and oooh…I was having an orgasm just looking at it! I couldn't wait to get inside and revel in it!

And strangely, it was completely empty! There were no guests in it at all - it was like a private sauna created just for me. I couldn't understand how this lovely thing could be empty - maybe the trekking season was petering out or something…but there were enough people on the road - we had been bumping into a lot of them.

But what did I care? I just shrugged and accepted it as a gift from God - a present for having bravely done the EBC trek. I went to the mens section and Bharathi went to women's and I stripped off and went - AAAAAH - as I entered the sauna and felt the delicious heat relaxing and unwinding my tired muscles. What a wonderful feeling! Bliss!

> O! Water cold we may pour at need
> down a thirsty throat and be glad
indeed;
> but better is Beer, if drink we lack,
> and Water Hot poured down the back.

> O! Water is fair that leaps on high
> in a fountain white beneath the sky;
> but never did fountain sound so sweet
> as splashing Hot Water with my feet!

Then I entered the jacuzzi and again went - AAAAH - as the swirling jets of water hit me and massaged my kinks away. I lay there for several minutes, and  - maybe it was the stimulating effects of the jets of water - I suddenly became…thoughtful. The thought struck me that the place was totally empty!

A ha!

The mens and women's sections were separated by a common wall, and I whispered to Bharathi and asked her if there was anybody with her. No, she replied. She was totally alone!

A ha!

The thought of her being alone in that shower really enthused me, and I thought that I should join her. For a friendly…er… chat.

A ha!

I crept out of the mens room and walked to the women's section, dripping wet and ready for chatting! Bharathi was waiting expectantly for me, and we were going to…

BAM!

I walked full-speed and head-first into a pillar!

OW! OW! OW! OW!

Earlier a thought had struck me, and now the pillar struck me! I had hit my head so hard, that I blacked out for a second.

Stars lit up in front of my eyes, and there was ringing in my ears! I was totally disoriented! What the fuck just happened? I staggered and slipped and fell on my ass.

Slip! THUD!

OW! OW! OW!

I lay there for a second in the darkness, dazedly wondering who I was and where I was and what was I doing on the floor, dripping wet in the dark. If I had been in a cartoon, there would have birds flying and tweeting in a circle around my head.

Then I remembered. Oh yeah. Chatting!

I got up and shambled blindly into the women's section where she was waiting for me expectantly.

'What happened to you?'

'Nothing. Nothing…ah, where were we?'

A ha!

## Lukla to Kathmandu

Well, here we were. The trek was over and the only thing that remained was to catch a flight back to Kathmandu.

We stayed in bed till late - me rubbing my sore head - watching the flights take off and land on that ridiculously small runway. It was most exciting - the runway is actually at an angle (there is no really flat land anywhere in those mountains. The runway must have been built on flattish land, or the nearest approximation to flat land they could find) and the planes come and land on that slope and taxi up - literally up the slope - to the airport.

We finally got up and had breakfast and then strolled over to the airport to buy tickets. But it was so strange - there seemed to be nobody there to sell us tickets! The whole place was empty. Finally we found one guy inside the airport who sold us tickets - and had the surreal experience of bargaining the price. I had never bargained for an air ticket before and found the experience fascinating! He started by asking for a 100 USD, and I scoffed at him and we went back and forth, and finally I spoke to him in hindi and he gave the tickets for 48 USD!

As we waited for our flight, I was thinking of how this airport came to be. It was because of Edmund Hillary's philanthropy. Hillary is intensely respected in Nepal and especially in the SoluKhumbu region - not just because he was the first guy to climb Everest, but because of his kind heart and good works.

After that first ascent in 1953, Hillary made several trips to Nepal (one of which was an expedition to find the Yeti - the Abominable snowman. They searched high and low and investigated foot prints and alleged bits and pieces of Yetis preserved in monasteries - skulls, bones, paws, pelts etc) and finally came to the unsurprising and unromantic conclusion that it did not exist) and he really wanted to do something for the people of Nepal, and give back to the community that he loved so much.

One day at a high camp during an expedition in 1960, he asked his Sirdar what, above all, would he like for his children and the Sherpa people. ...the sirdar asked for a school in his village of Khumjung.

Hillary thought about how to go about it - what would be the best and most practical and long lasting way to do it - and then decided to open a trust - The Himalayan Trust - an international non-profit humanitarian organisation to improve the health, education and general wellbeing of people living in the Solukhumbu District. The Himalayan Trust would operate from New Zealand and work through partnerships with local NGOs in Nepal and focus on building sustainable infrastructure for the benefit of the local people.

By 1961 the first school was built in the Khumbu region of Nepal, as the first major project of the Himalayan Trust.

The following year Sir Ed received requests for two more schools, one from Thame and one from Pangboche. The letter from Thame read:

27 October 1962

Sir

Respected Bara Sahib Sir Edmund Hillary

We the local people, the Sherpas of Thame, Khumbu, came to know that your honour, helping us in all respects, is going to open some more schools in Khumbu. So we Thame people are requesting your honour to open a school at Thame just like Khumjung. Though our children have eyes but still they are blind! So all we Sherpas of Thame are praying your honour to make our children just like those of Khumjung. We hope your honour may consider our prayer.

Yours,

Chewang Rimpi Sherpa

Thak Noori Sherpa

Kinken Kang Sherpa

Khunjo Chumbi Sherpa

Both schools were completed in 1963 along with other Himalayan Trust projects.

Since then the Himalayan trust has

carried out a number of projects for the benefit of the people in the Solu khumbu region - schools, water pipelines and water management, health, sanitation and immunisation, earthquake relief etc. More than 30 schools have been built by the trust. Hillary remained the chairman of the trust till his death, and he is still loved and respected throughout the place. I saw a number of signboards on the trail hailing Sir Ed as 'Father of the Khumbu region'.

By 1964, it was clear to Edmund Hillary that the transport of building materials to the high regions needed to be easier, so the Himalayan Trust built an airstrip. The site chosen was beside the tiny village of Lukla - and this is now the second busiest airstrip in Nepal!

In January 2008 the Lukla Airport was renamed as the 'Tenzing–Hillary Airport' in recognition of their promotion of its construction - and I was sitting in that same airport.

As we entered the plane, I also realised that we had been extremely lucky! Because of the trickiness of the tiny airstrip and mountainous neighbourhood, the flights are extremely dependant on the weather and can easily get cancelled if there is any chance of bad weather. Trekkers have been stuck here for days and days, waiting for the weather to clear.

But we had no problems - the only thing was the moment of heart-stopping terror when that tiny plane hurtles down the slope and jumps off into the valley - AAAAARGGGHHHH - WE ARE GOING TO DIE! - Before the plane rights itself and takes wing.

I enjoyed myself looking down into the valleys and mountains - what had taken us 6 days to walk was covered by the plane in half an hour!

I could imagine all the trekkers toiling up the roads below, and enjoying the views as we had enjoyed them. Trekking is great for the trekker, obviously - and it is also the breath of life to the country due to the employment and revenue that it generates for the local people. And it is amazing to think that the whole concept of 'Trekking' here is very modern - it started just in the 1960s.

While the world was pre-occupied with Everest fever in that 'age of achievements and record breaking' - the momentum slowly shifted from watching the feats of explorers and adventurers to people wanting to explore the mountains for themselves. Normal people wanted to see these amazing mountains and landscapes, and meet the smiling and picturesque people - without wanted to actually climb the high mountains. They would be happy to just see the 8000ers from up close - even if they did not have the ability to climb the summits. This led to development of trekking as an international phenomenon.

To be sure, the Himalaya captured the imagination of travellers long before the present trekking boom began, and even in the late 19th and early years of the 20th century local agents in Kashmir, Simla and Darjeeling were already equipping parties eager to get close to the highest mountains and to cross some of their passes. Adventurous people wanted to go there for various reasons - hunting and shooting, scientific study, hunting for rare plants and flowers which would fetch fantastic prices in the west, exploring unknown areas - and of course, mountaineering. But some people just wanted to come and see the place - with no other agenda.

One of the first to be drawn to the mountains of what was then British India was Alpine Club stalwart Douglas Freshfield who, in 1899, made a seven-week tour of the Kangchenjunga massif in very difficult conditions along with Italian Photographer Vittorio Sella. Freshfield was a British lawyer who was a mountain and adventure lover, and he was a member of the Royal Geographical society and the Alpine club - and became founder and first president of the Geographical society. He wrote a book about his travels in the Himalayas called 'Round Kanchenjunga', in which he wrote about Dzongri -

' Suddenly you are in the presence of the Snow mountain unless they are indeed as they seem, in the first awestruck moment of beholding, embodied spirits of overwhelming power and malignity. Below you is the Prague Chu Valley; before you on the other side, long line of mountains-a succession of terrible granite spires, running down, one and all so steep and jagged that it seems as if no snow could ever cling to their sides. They have been fearfully searched by winds that mark the course in sweep of the wrinkled drifts and all the scars and lines run downwards giving the mountains an infinitely cheerless and depreciating expression like a sad, worn face.'

At the western end of the Himalaya, the American couple Robert and Katherine

Barrett spent a year wandering through Baltistan and Ladakh in 1923-24 with Rasul Galwan from Leh as their sirdar. They published a book about their travels - 'The Himalayan letters of Gypsy Dave and Lady Ba written on pilgrimage to the high quiet places among the simple people of an old folk tale.'

    Their sirdar - Rasool Galwan - was one of the most interesting personalities among the guides of the day. He was the grandson of a most famous thief - a 'Robin Hood' kind of character who was called 'Kara Galwan' - or 'The black thief' and he was so bold that he even entered the bedroom of the King of Kashmir and threatened him with a knife and told him to stop hunting for him, or he would be back and the knife would be for more than show! But later the Kara Galwan was caught by treachery and then hanged.

Rasool Galwan was brought up in poverty, but then created a famous career as one of the most famous guides and sirdars of the Ladakh Himalayas. He worked with big names such as Francis Younghusband, Lord Dunnore, Sven Hedin and the scientific expeditions of Fellipo Filipi. He was so respected by the expedition leaders that they named a river after him - the Galwan river, which flows out of Aksai Chin in what is now China Occupied Kashmir (COK).

When he met the Barrets, the American couple were so impressed with him that they encouraged him to write a book in his own words. Galwan plunged into the affair and wrote a book - in English! A most remarkable feat for a self taught mountain boy in the primitive Ladakh of that times! The Barrets edited it a bit, but left it more or less the way he wrote it - in pidgin English, but straight from the heart - and this was published as 'Servant of Sahibs - A book to read aloud'.

(It is a most remarkable piece of work - I found an online copy - check it out here- https://archive.org/details/in.ernet.dli.2015.173801 )

Rasool Galwan described the Barrett's journey: 'No, not shooting; not rocks-collecting, not flowers keeping; not heads measuring, not mountains measuring; not pictures taking. This my Sahib and Mem-Sahib travelling where their felt are liked, camping always high place to look the country.'

Decipher that, and you'll find another definition of trekking.

The Barretts travelled in style, their outfit

luxurious. They slept in handsome embroidered tents, travelled with eight servants to look after their needs, and had no fewer than 20 ponies and a team of porters to carry their supplies. They lacked nothing. This was much like the posh camping trips of our Swiss and European friends - where they travelled in style with a whole bunch of guides, porters and cooks.

Bill Tilman and Eric Shipton - of the first Everest recon mission in Nepal - were masters of lightweight travel - for a five-month expedition Shipton decided that two shirts would suffice. Tilman thought this excessive and took only one.

Shipton admitted that 'there is much to be said for a simple mountain journey, whose object, unencumbered with the burden of detailed map-making or scientific observation, is just to get from one place to another'.

That surely is another definition of trekking. And that was the kind of trekking that we cheapskate backpackers did - no porters, no guides…carry little, and carry it yourself.

The transport officer for the successful 1953 expedition that put Ed Hillary and Tenzing Norgay on Everest's summit was Jimmy Roberts, then a major in a Gurkha regiment and an experienced Himalayan climber. When he retired in the 1960s, he did not want to go back to England, but remained in Nepal in the shadow of Annapurna.

But what do do in Nepal ? He noticed that while high-altitude mountaineering could be a masochistic - not to mention expensive and dangerous - pursuit, the long walk to reach the foot of the mountains was one of stress-free enjoyment likely to appeal to adventurous travellers. Aha! Light bulb moment - why not start a business to help people trek to the base camp? It would be far easier than organising an assault on Everest, and there would be many more takers for it. And given his fame as a member of that famous Everest expedition, he would find it easy to get customers.

In 1964 he registered Mountain Travel as Nepal's first trekking agency, and the following year accompanied three American ladies on a springtime trek in the Khumbu - no doubt taking pains to point out to them that this was the self-same route which had been taken by them - and Hillary and Tenzing - on that famous expedition in 1953.

Trekking, as we know it today, was born - as was the Everest Base Camp trail!

I sighed as the plane bumped down in

Kathmandu airport.

Our trek was over. It was time to go home.

'The Road goes ever on and on
Out from the door where it began.
Now far ahead the Road has gone,
Let others follow it who can!
Let them a journey new begin,
But I at last with weary feet
Will turn towards the lighted inn,
My evening-rest and sleep to meet.'


We went back to our hotel in Thamel and Bharathi celebrated her return to civilisation by picking fights with a cycle rickshaw guy and a pay-phone guy and almost getting me beaten up!

It started with finding out that there was a strike on in Kathmandu that day, and no taxis were available. Sensible people would have stayed in a hotel near to the airport - but we decided to make our way to Thamel - nothing else would do! Thamel or bust!
Bharathi found a cycle-rickshaw guy who was willing to take us to Thamel.
'Cycle rickshaw? All the way to Thamel?' I said doubtfully, but she just waved my doubts away.

'TCHAH. TCHOOH. We should support these poor guys and give them the benefit of our custom!' she said grandly.

Poor guy? I thought to myself. This guy looks like a guy who makes his money ripping off clueless foreigners. But there was no point in arguing with her, so I got on.

Sure enough, as soon as there was an upslope anywhere, the guy would stop the rickshaw and make us get off and walk and cycle up much beyond the slope and laugh as we walked up. This was OK for the severe climbs, but soon he was making us get off just for kicks. Bharathi finally lost her cool and shouted at him and got off and made me get off as well.

'Well, I showed him!' she said grimly. 'I got off his rickshaw. Cheating bastard.'

'Showed him?' I said in disbelief 'You walked half the time, got off half way - and yet paid him for the full trip! He is the one who showed you!'

'NO NO, I SHOWED HIM!'

'I can see him there - see, there he is - laughing at us!'

And sure enough, that rogue came back and said 'Want to get on again? This time it will cost you double - HAHAHA'

'AARGH! GO AND FIGHT WITH HIM!' she ordered me, but I managed to pull her away.

We finally reached Thamel and checked back in the same guest house, and in the evening she went to a pay-phone shop to make a call to her home in Madras, India. But, as luck would have it, we ended up with a crooked phone operator.

Her phone call to India did not connect, but she was billed for it anyway - so she got into a huge fight with the boy there and refused to pay. I was standing quietly by the side and minding my own business - and nearly jumped out of my skin when that guy turned on me!

'I can't beat up the girl - so I will beat you up instead!'

'What? What?' I yammered and nearly shit my pants.

This was like the scene in Asterix where Fulliautomatix punches Cacofonix in the face because he couldn't bring himself to punch old Geriatrix.

'Yes! Yes!' the little titch screamed. 'Beat him up! Beat him up!'

This caused both of us - me and that guy - to pause in confusion, wondering who exactly was to be beaten up. My head was still sore from walking into the pillar, and so I was greatly relieved when the owner of the shop intervened and calmed things down. I was in love - but not enough to get beaten up for her.

I was loathe to let our time end, and so I dumped my flight back to Bombay! It would get me into severe hot water at home and in office -but it would give me 3 days more with Bharathi.

We spent our time chilling out in Kathmandu - and discovered many interesting things - such as that one should not eat spicy food before…er… chatting - else unfortunate results can ensue … requiring the use of very cold water, and that beds in cheap backpacker hostels are not as sturdy as they should be and if the so called 'double bed' is actually two single beds put together rather than a single large bed …they can drift apart and cause you to end up on the floor in a most undignified position at an unfortunate time, and if you want to imitate a romantic movie and throw a girl on a bed…you should ensure that it is a fancy bed with a deep mattress and not one with a paper-thin mattress where the impact will knock the breath out of her and almost break her back!

We also discovered that the anticipation of loss can be worse than loss itself. We kept thinking that our magical time was over - and soon we would part, soon we would part, soon we would…and this actually was a dampener on the time we were together. Dammit.

The time finally come to actually part now - we were booked on separate flights - me to Bombay and she to Chennai, where she could relax and decompress after her travels. What would she do now? Her plans were still fluid - she was still on her sabbatical and had many things in mind. She was thinking about a rafting trip on the Ganga and a cycling expedition of 600 kilometres from Goa to Trivandum. Would I like to come?

I winced and tightened my ass. I had been on a short ride once, and my perineum had pained for days because the thin end of the unyielding cycle seat cruelly bruised my tender parts! I walked like a duck for days after a single days ride -  so  - no!

Also, she would have to do job-hunting soon - and I knew this would be a very difficult and emotionally bruising time for her. Sabbaticals are not appreciated in India, and she would definitely have trouble convincing hirers that she was not a madwoman or an eccentric - or worse.

She was open to relocating anywhere in India -  and god knows where she would end up - and God only knew what would happen to 'us'.

But now I was relaxed about it, and left such questions to fate. Que sera sera and all that - what will be, will bloody well be, and there was no point in getting worked up about it.

Didn't God give me this EBC trek, when it was the absolute last thing on my mind?

And it had turned out to be one of the greatest experiences of my life. So - keep an open mind, and see what turns up.

As we parted, she looked at me and promised that we would meet again. How and where and what will do was something yet to be seen …

She was a force of nature, and would be carrying me along with her!

I could see that Life was going to be interesting from here on.

Bring it on!

### Before you go…

Thanks so much for reading my book!

If you liked it, **please do consider leaving a rating and a review** on Amazon and Goodreads. This would be a great help to me and the book - Thanks!

It would also be great if you could tell your friends about the book and spread the word on your social networks- self-published authors need all the help we can get :)

Do check out my site for all my books, photos and videos - and my blog. Please do feel free to write into me and let me know what you thought of the book.

# www.ketanjoshi.net
Photo galleries. Blog. Contact me

**Check out the 1st book in this series**
ONE MAN GOES BACKPACKING
The Amigo @ the Kumbh Mela

Have you checked out my other books?

THREE MEN ON MOTORCYCLES -
The Amigos ride to Ladakh

THREE MEN RIDE AGAIN -
The Amigos ride to Spiti

THREE MEN RIDE SOUTH -
The Amigos ride to Coorg

THREE MEN RIDE THE CLIFFHANGER -
The Amigos ride the most dangerous roads in the world

THREE MEN RIDE WEST -
The Amigos ride to Gujarat and Diu

**Do Check out these Thrilling Fiction books as well**

BOMBAY THRILLERS
DIPY SINGH - PRIVATE DETECTIVE
DIPY SINGH - THE MYSTERY OF THE OFFICE RAT

Printed in Great Britain
by Amazon